# Through Chord-Melody&

## HOWARD MORGEN

**How to Access the Videos and Printable PDFs on the Enhanced CD**
Place the CD in your computer's CD-ROM drive.

Windows: Double-click on My Computer, then right-click on your CD drive icon and select Explore. You will see two folders: "Videos" and "Printable PDFs." Open the appropriate folder to view the files you want. Double-click on a file to view it immediately, or save it to a folder on your hard drive to view later.

Mac: Double-click on the CD volume named "Howard_Morgen" on your desktop. You will see two folders: "Videos" and "Printable PDFs." Open the appropriate folder to view the files you want. Double-click on a file to view it immediately, or save it to a folder on your hard drive to view later.

Songs and worksheets with printable PDF files are indicated throughout the book with this logo:

**Acknowledgements**
This project is dedicated to my wife, Estelle, my tireless sounding board and super-typist; to my editor, Aaron Stang, who suggested the idea for the book and who shepherded it through to its successful conclusion; and to Howard Alden—a guitarist's guitarist. Thank you.

**Credits**
Managing Editor: Aaron Stang
Text Editors: Aaron Stang, Jack Allen, Kate Westin
Book Layout and Music Engraving: Mark Burgess
Production Editor: Donny Trieu
Cover Design: Ted Engelbart
Interior Photos: Jack Huntley
Cover Photo: Gary Morgen
Videographer: Davis Stillson
Audio Recording: Howard Morgen, Howard Alden

**Alfred Music**
P.O. Box 10003
Van Nuys, CA 91410-0003
alfred.com

ISBN-10: 0-7390-4984-4 (Book & CD)
ISBN-13: 978-0-7390-4984-6 (Book & CD)

2

# Contents

*(V) indicates that a video performance by Howard Morgen is available on your enhanced CD.*

*Note: All 19 full song arrangements are available as printable PDFs on your enhanced CD.*

# Note from the Author

You're an intermediate level player or beyond. You play in a band or you play alone for your own enjoyment. You love to listen to and, on occasion, have played through guitar arrangements featured in specialty magazines and folios. You'd even love to arrange a few tunes yourself...

If you fit into any of these categories, chances are you already know enough to start creating your own arrangements and, what you don't know, you can pick up along the way. What you need are step-by-step procedures that help you get started and successful experiences with the arranging process that will give you the confidence to keep going. You'll also need to experience these procedures first hand, so, wherever possible, I've given you that hands-on opportunity.

Over the years, my goal has always been to produce books, articles, and arrangements that suggest approaches for creating one's own arrangements. For a solo performer in the jazz idiom, that's where the art is. Some of the topics that are introduced in this book have never before appeared in any of my previous work while other topics that have appeared before are now revealed in a new context and with a new focus.

*Through Chord-Melody and Beyond* is a summary and synthesis of much of what I have learned about arranging for guitar and it is my hope that it will prove to be a valuable contribution to your musical progress and development.

Howard Morgen

# Introduction

This book is intended for intermediate to advanced players as an overview, guide, and sourcebook. It is written in two parts and contains both standard notation and TAB. Plus, note-for-note performances are included on the companion CD.

Playing solo guitar, like playing solo piano, means self-accompaniment. Part 1 (Chapters 1–5) focuses on five jazz-oriented approaches to self-accompaniment:

- chord-melody style

- chord-melody derivations

- comping below a single melody line

- comping above a single melody line

- walking bass lines

Part 2 (Chapters 6–14) is devoted to supplying the theoretical information, harmonic concepts, thought processes, and techniques that are the essential underpinnings of all successful arrangements.

Throughout the book, 11 classic jazz standards from Alfred's *Just Jazz Real Book* are employed as examples and exercises and as complete, fully developed arrangements demonstrating the entire range of topics presented. At the end of each chapter, you will find a "Guide List" that references topically related works of other authors that will supply you with additional information, perspectives, and insights.

## Some Suggestions for Approaching the Material

*Through Chord-Melody and Beyond* can be both a source book and a guide using the table of contents to create your own study plan according to your own needs and by investigating the related works of recommended authors and books cited on the guide lists.

Depending on your present knowledge of musical terminology, basic theory, previous arranging experience and playing level, the chapters may be approached either sequentially or non-sequentially. For example, an intermediate level player unfamiliar with musical terminology would benefit with back-to-back study of Chapter 1 (an overview of chord-melody style) and Chapter 6 (a discussion of musical terminology used in this book). In fact, many chapters in both Parts 1 and 2 may be studied simultaneously since the overview of the five jazz-oriented approaches to self-accompaniment outlined and demonstrated in Part 1 and the detailed discussion of their theoretical conception and technical underpinnings are two sides of the same coin.

You'll find it helpful before beginning the study of any of the fully developed arrangements to first listen to the note-for-note performances on the companion CD while following along with the standard notation and TAB.

## About the Songs

All the song titles were written during the "golden age" of popular songwriting, a period when melody and harmony were king. Tastes in popular music are always changing, and, over time, many lovers of popular music either haven't heard these songs performed or have come to associate them in a negative way with the vapid, watered-down versions occasionally piped in to elevators, shopping malls, and dentist's offices—ouch!

Fortunately, the advent of the internet and sophisticated digital home recording equipment are making it possible to access, download, record, compile, and own (at a very nominal cost) music from this period, including original performances and exciting, vibrant interpretations by a wide variety of singers and instrumentalists. I recommend that, before going further, you take advantage of this technology and familiarize yourself with at least two or three versions of each of the song titles listed below. Listen to singers rather than instrumentalists first because you will then get to hear the song's lyric as well as its original melody. (Jazz players often feel that knowing a song's lyric can really help with its interpretation.) In addition to purchasing CDs, you can easily go online and download classic versions of these songs from many commercial websites such as iTunes.*

The following songs are used as examples in this book:

| | |
|---|---|
| "'Round Midnight" | "It's Only a Paper Moon" |
| "Li'l Darlin'" | "My Funny Valentine" |
| "The More I See You" | "Body and Soul" |
| "Stardust" | "My Foolish Heart" |
| "Alone Together" | "Nice Work If You Can Get It" |
| "Speak Low" | |

*\* To purchase songs from a legitimate music website, go to any of the established providers such as Amazon.com (select the Music tab) or iTunes.com (for iTunes you will need to download the free iTunes software before you can purchase songs). Type the name of the song and/or artist into the search field. A list of songs matching the search criteria will appear. You may preview songs with a brief excerpt before buying. To buy the song, hit the purchase button. If you are a first-time customer, you will be guided through the process of opening an account and creating a unique customer ID and password. After that, the song will be downloaded to your computer and will appear in the song lists (play lists) of your computer's default digital media player (iTunes, Windows Media Player, Rhapsody, etc.).*

# Important Information for Notation Non-Readers

As you progress through this book, it is important to carefully examine the standard notation that appears directly above the TAB you are playing. TAB gives you fret and string locations for all the notes, but it does not provide the visual information you need to do the following:

1. Separate and keep track of melody, chords, and bass parts.
   This information is more easily recognized in the standard notation by the direction of the note stems. Notice the following in the Example below:

   - Note stems of the melody (top voice) are placed to the right of the notehead and point upward.

   - Note stems of the chord accompaniment (middle voice) are placed to the left of the notehead and point downward.

   - Note stems of the bass part (bottom voice) are placed to the left of the notehead and point downward.

**Example 1:**
Standard Notation for Guitar Illustrating Three Independent Parts of Melody,
Chord Accompaniment, and Bass

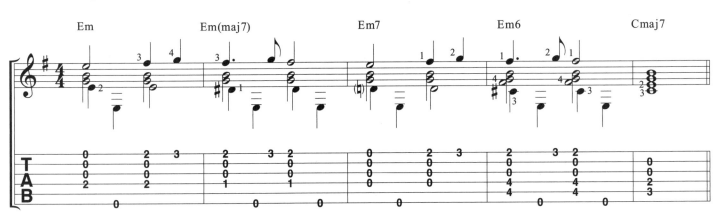

2. Determine how long any given note or chord is to be sustained.
   In standard notation, the shape of the notehead in conjunction with its accompanying note stem indicates how long any note or chord is sustained.

| note | | duration | count |
|---|---|---|---|
| ♪ (♪) | = eighth note | one-half beat | (count expressed in lowest common denominator of eighth note) |
| ♫ | = two eighth notes | one full beat | 1 & |
| ♩ | = quarter note | one full beat | 1 & |
| ♩. | = dotted quarter note | one and a half beats | 1 & 2 |
| ♩ | = half note | two full beats | 1 & 2 & |
| ♩. | = dotted half note | three full beats | 1 & 2 & 3 & |
| o | = whole note | four full beats | 1 & 2 & 3 & 4 & |

3. Know the exact beat on which any note or chord is sounded.
   In standard notation, the time a note or chord is sounded is indicated by its placement within the measure in relation to the count.

**Example 2**

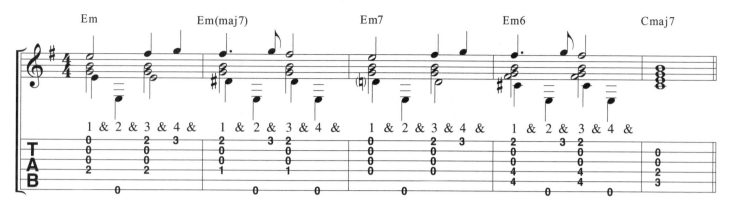

In case you are not familiar with solo guitar notation, here is a complete step-by-step breakdown of measure 1 of the above example.

**On count 1:**

- Melody note E (up-stemmed half note) is sounded and sustained for two full beats (1 & 2 &).

- Chord accompaniment notes B and G (down-stemmed half notes) are sounded and sustained for two full beats (1 & 2 &).

- Bass note E (down-stemmed quarter note) is sounded and sustained for one full beat (1 &).

**On count 2:**

- Bass note low E (down-stemmed quarter note) is sounded and sustained for one full beat (2 &).

**On count 3:**

- Melody note F# (up-stemmed quarter note) is sounded for one full beat (3 &).

- Chord accompaniment notes B and G (down-stemmed half notes) are sounded and sustained for two full beats (3 & 4 &).

- Bass note E (down-stemmed half note) is sounded and sustained for two full beats (3 & 4 &).

**On count 4:**

- Note G (up-stemmed quarter note) is sounded and sustained for one full beat (4 &).

4. Select practical fingerings for the fretting hand.

# PART 1:

# Approaches to Self-Accompaniment for Solo Jazz Guitar

# Chapter 1:
# Chord-Melody Style

The term "chord-melody" was coined at a time when most pop and jazz guitar styles called for either single-note melody lines rooted in a horn-like concept or straight, percussive, chord accompaniment. Guitarists began using the term chord-melody to refer to an early approach to solo guitar in which both the melody and its related chord harmony are sounded simultaneously as a single "block" chord structure with the melody voiced on top of the chord shape. See Example 3.

**Example 3**

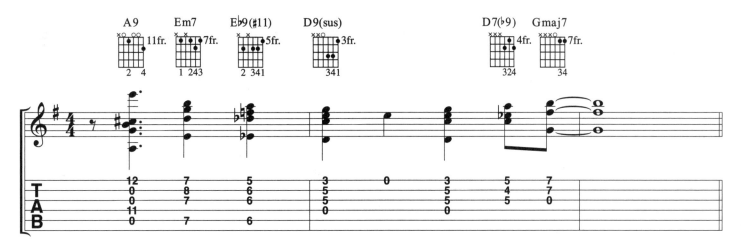

Although fingered as a single chord shape, at least two parts (melody and accompaniment) are usually implied in standard notation with the note stems of the melody pointing upward and the note stems of the accompaniment pointing downward, as shown here.

**Example 3a**

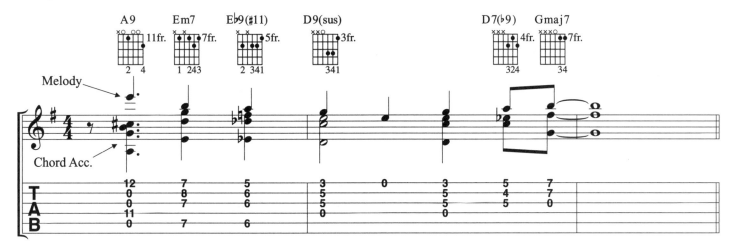

## Setting Up a Chord-Melody Style Arrangement

Below is a lead sheet containing the melody and chord symbols for the first eight measures of "My Funny Valentine."

**Example 4**

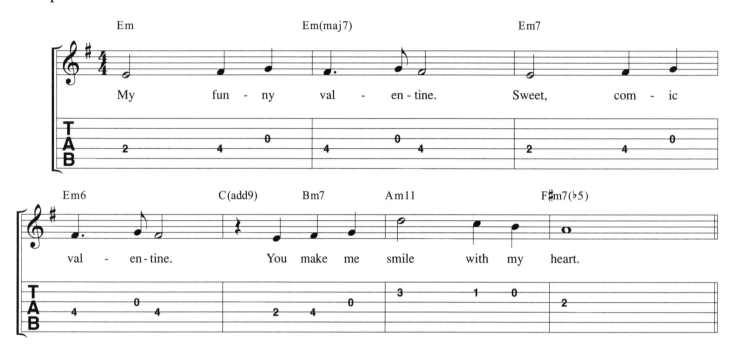

In chord-melody style, the melody part is voiced as the top note of the chord structure so that it will stand out as the chord is sounded.

## Step 1: Transposing the Melody Note Up One Octave

In order to provide room on the fingerboard for chord placement below the melody, you usually need to transpose the melody note **up one octave** from where it appears on the lead sheet. Here is the melody of "My Funny Valentine" raised one octave from the lead sheet and relocated along the 1st and 2nd strings.

**Example 4a**

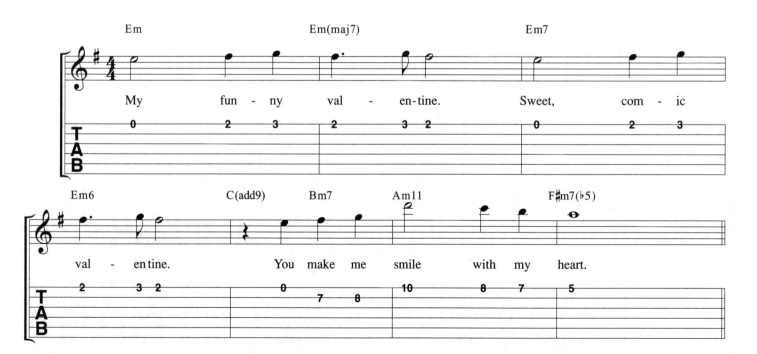

## Step 2: Choosing Chord Voicings for Placement Below the Melody

When the melody is a chord tone, there are usually a number of potential voicings that will "work" depending on the location of the melody note on the fingerboard. See the following examples.

Chord = Am7
Melody note G located on the 1st string, 3rd fret.

Chord = Am7
Melody note G located on the 2nd string, 8th fret.

When the melody note is a non-chord tone (not part of the chord):

1.  Look for the nearest available chord tone that lies *directly below* the non-chord tone and form a voicing with that chord tone on top.
2.  Retain the chord shape while replacing the top chord tone with the non-chord tone melody note.

In the figure below, see how we take a non-chord tone (B) and use it to replace the top note (A) in the Am7 chord shape.

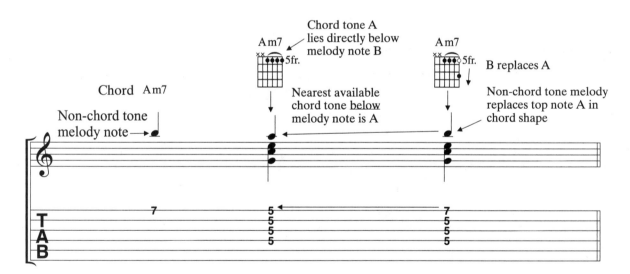

## Step 3: Placing the Chord Voicings

Most chord-melody style arrangements combine chords (usually played on strong beats) with single notes (played on weak beats). The following is a hands-on demonstration of the process of searching for and choosing a chord voicing and placing it below a melody note.

Example 5 is a worksheet displaying the melody and chord symbols for the first seven measures of "My Funny Valentine." The up-stemmed melody part has already been transposed up one octave from the lead sheet as in Example 4A and is located along the 1st and 2nd strings. The chord symbols are placed directly over the melody notes that will become the top voices of those chords.

Procedure: Based on the chord symbol designations located above the melody part, choose your chord shapes from among the randomly located chord grids that follow, and place each shape directly below its corresponding melody note. The top note of the voicing you choose *must correspond in pitch and fret location to the melody note you are harmonizing on the worksheet.* After completing this example, check your results with Example 6.

Note: When writing solo guitar arrangements the top part (usually the melody) is written with stems up and the bottom part (usually the bass line) with stems down. Middle parts might be attached to either the upper or lower part—or may be written independently with stems either up or down—depending on what is the clearest method for the situation.

**Example 5**

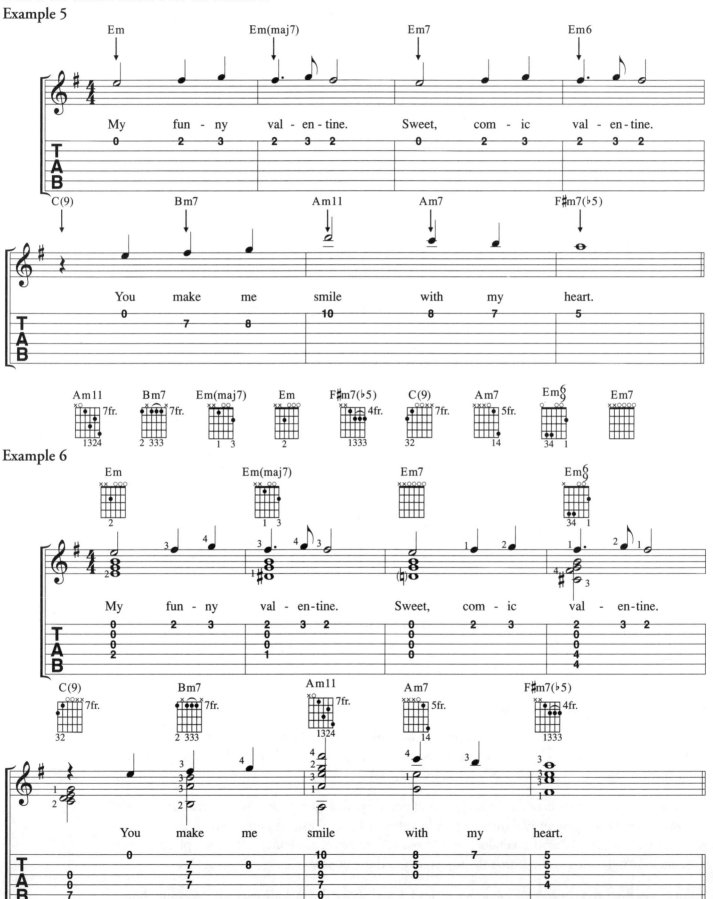

**Example 6**

# Chord-Melody Exercises 1a–1e

The following exercises include worksheets with excerpts of the melody and chords from five classic "standards" along with the chord symbols and chord grids needed to complete each exercise. The melody parts in each exercise have already been raised one octave and located along the upper three strings to accommodate the chord voicings.

Procedure: As in Example 5, select the needed chord shapes indicated by the chord symbols from among the randomly located chord grids and place each voicing below its corresponding melody note.

Note: Some chords occur where no melody notes are present—either on a rest or during a sustained melody note. The entire voicing designated by the chord symbol on that beat is to be sounded as part of the implied chord accompaniment and notated with down-stems. This occurs in the following exercises:

With rests:
>Exercise 1b, measure 4, Em7
>Exercise 1c, measure 3, Dm7
>Exercise 1d, measure 2, G7(♭13); measure 4, A7(♭13)

With sustained melody notes:
>Exercise 1c, measure 2, A7(♭9); measure 4, A7
>Exercise 1e, measure 2, D9; measure 4, A♯dim7

With second note of two tied notes sustained:
>Exercise 1b, measure 2, F♯m7
>Exercise 1d, measure 1, E♭maj7

When completed, check your results against Examples 7a–7e.

### Exercise 1a: Stardust

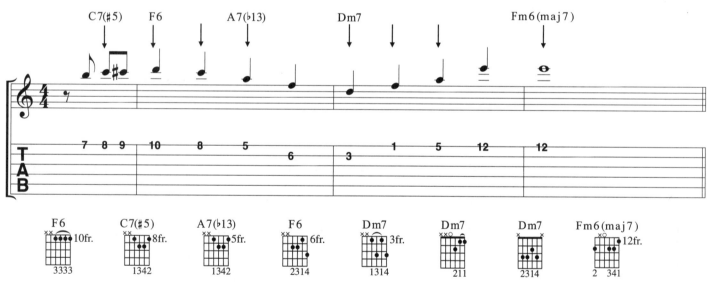

## Exercise 1b: The More I See You

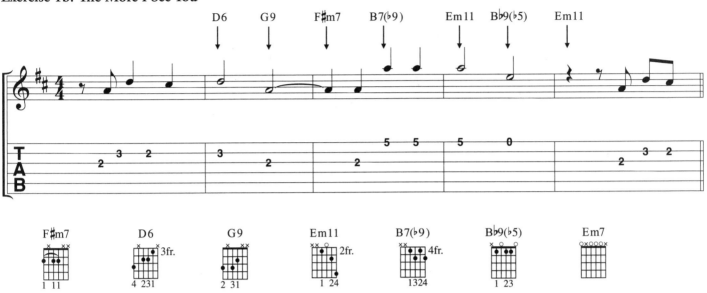

## Exercise 1c: Alone Together

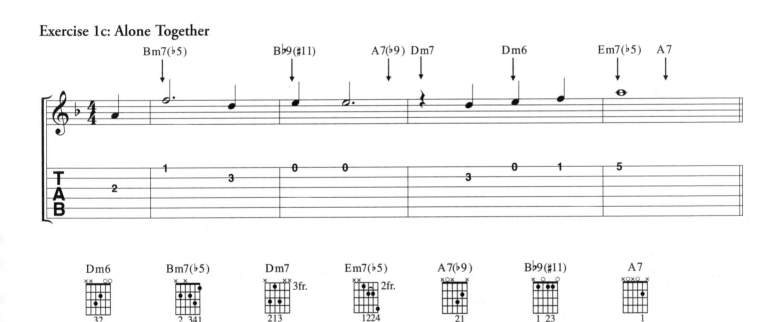

## Exercise 1d: My Foolish Heart

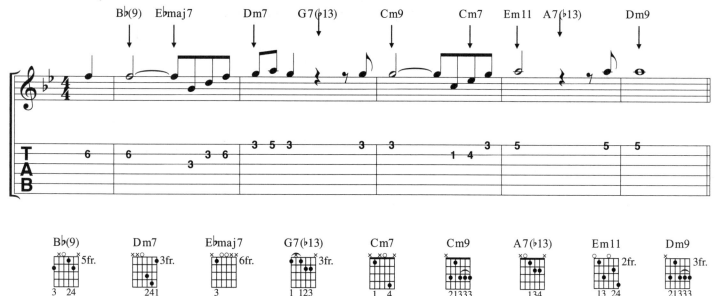

## Exercise 1e: Nice Work If You Can Get It

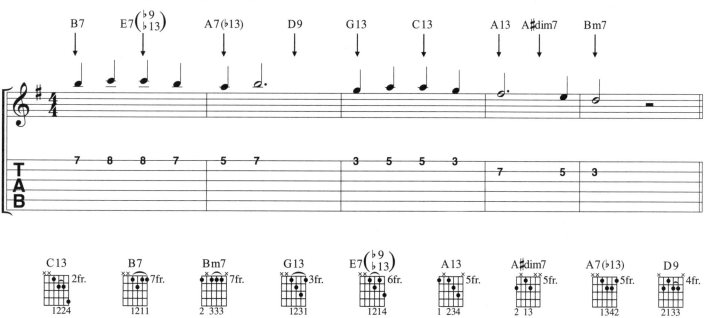

**Example 7a: Stardust**

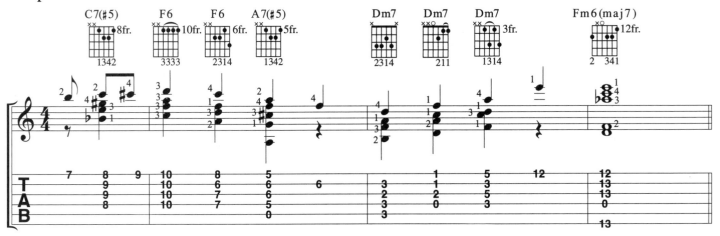

**Example 7b: The More I See You**

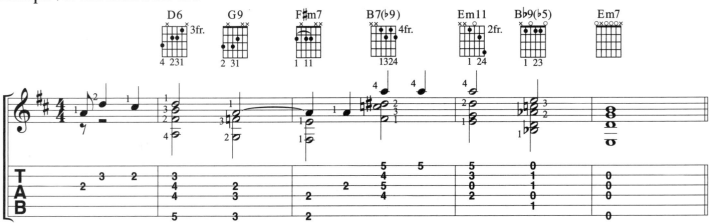

**Example 7c: Alone Together**

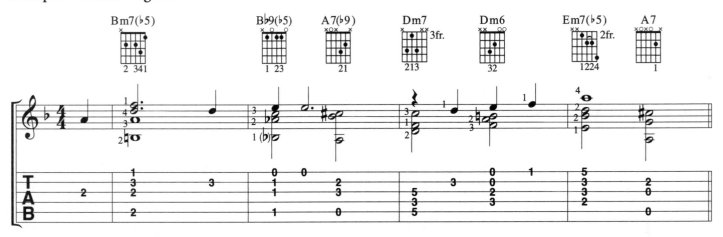

**Example 7d: My Foolish Heart**

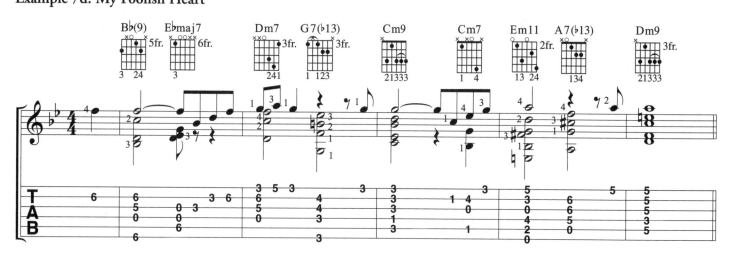

**Example 7e: Nice Work If You Can Get It**

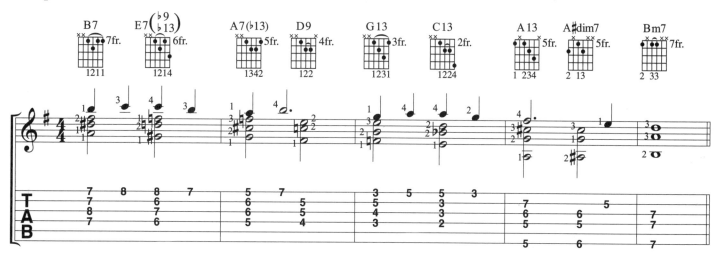

18

Neil Hefti's "Li'l Darlin'" is a perfect vehicle for a traditional "block" chord-melody style treatment like the one that follows. Play with a pick, pick-and-fingers, or fingerstyle.

If you play this arrangement with a pick, mute any voicing that contains a skipped open string by lightly touching the open string with the fleshy part of a fretting-hand finger.

# LI'L DARLIN'

By
NEAL HEFTI
*Arranged by*
*HOWARD MORGEN*

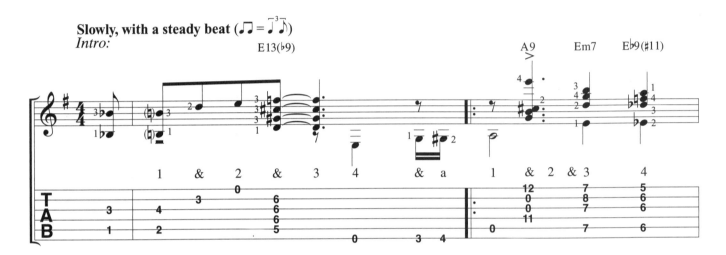

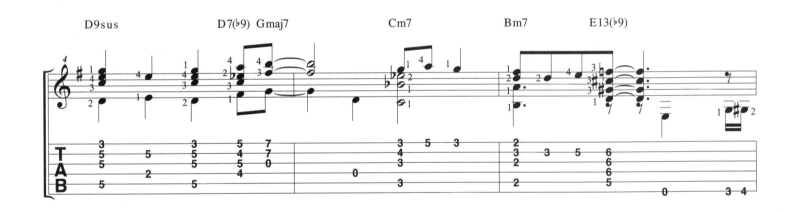

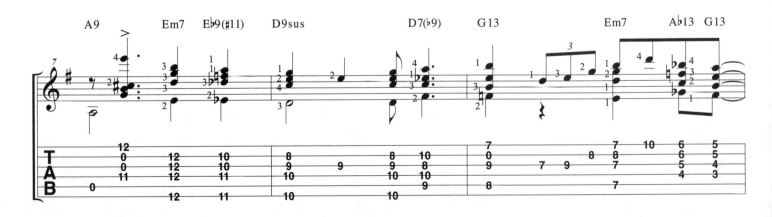

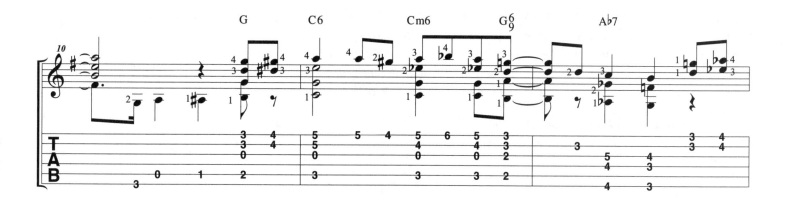

2nd time To Coda ⊕

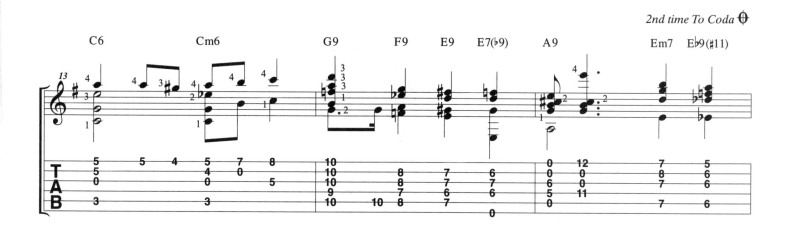

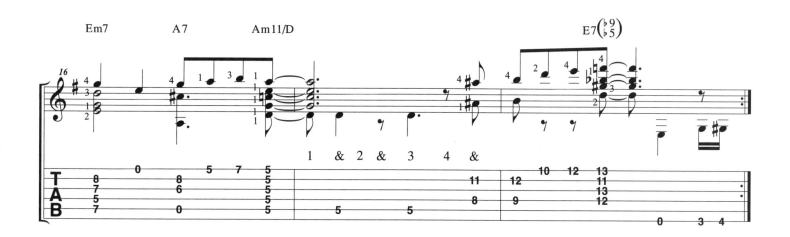

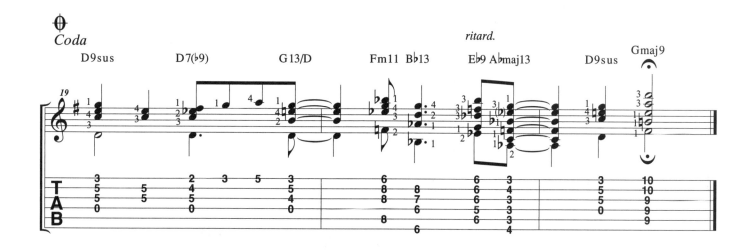

"Stardust," version no. 1 is a chord-melody treatment that can be played with a pick, pick and fingers, or fingerstyle. Throughout the arrangement, the majority of melody notes supported by chords are played on strong beats and single-note melody lines are played on both strong and weak beats (the exception to this occurs in measure 14 where a D9 is anticipated as a syncopation on the "& of 2" and in the next to the final measure of the coda where a G13(♭9) is played on the "& of 4" at the end of a ritard).

Note also in measures 11 and 12 how the chord voicings are held as their chord tones are sounded as an arpeggio. This approach to chord-melody is discussed in Chapter 2.

# STARDUST
## (Version 1)

Music by
HOAGY CARMICHAEL
Words by
MITCHELL PARISH
*Arranged by*
*HOWARD MORGEN*

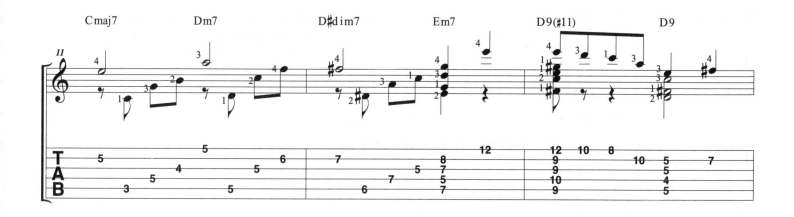

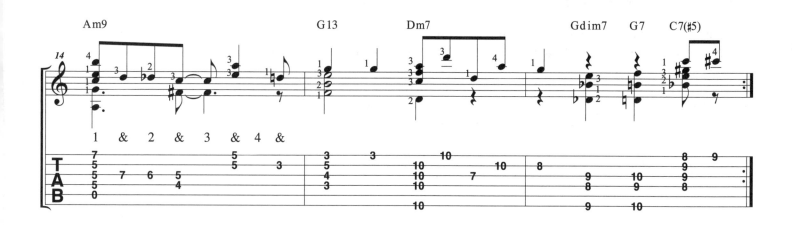

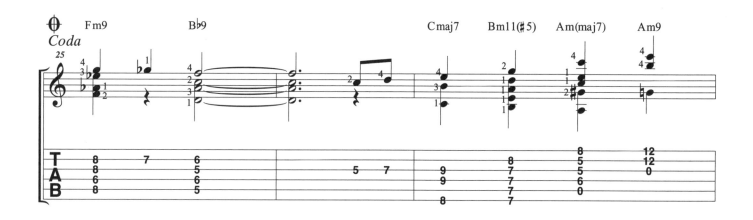

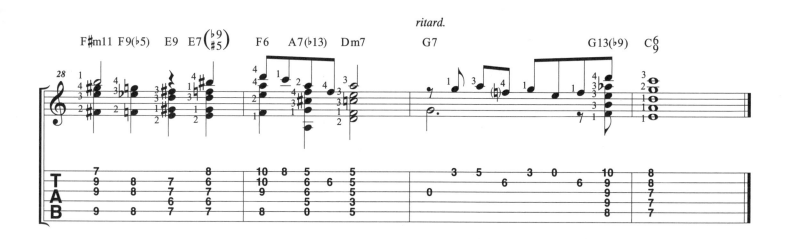

# Guide List for Chapter 1

See the Master Guide List at the end of the book for publisher and item number information for each book.

### *The Art of Solo Guitar Book 1*, Jody Fisher
Harmonizing a tune, playing and reading two parts, pages 47–48, 56–59.

### *Complete Jazz Guitar Method: Mastering Jazz Guitar: Chord/Melody*, Jody Fisher
Chord-melody procedures, pages 8–21.

### *Drop-2 Concept for Guitar*, Charles Chapman
Chord-melody procedures, pages 66–85.

### *Jazz Guitar for Classical Cats: Chord/Melody*, Andrew York
Basic chord-melody style with triads, pages 5–13.

### *The Jazz Guitar Chord Bible Complete*, Warren Nunes
A complete guide to three- and four-note voicings, including passing and altered chords.


## More Advanced Chord-Melody Concepts

### *Solo Jazz Guitar Method*, Barry Greene
Harmonizing a melody, harmonizing non-chord tones, pages 14–18.

### *Chord Chemistry*, Ted Greene
Chord-melody voicings for the blues, pages 94–103.

# Chapter 2:
# Chord-Melody Derivations

## Jazz Fingerstyle Technique

The adoption of classical fingerstyle technique by many jazz guitarists along with adaptations like pick-and-finger technique, thumb-pick and fingers, and tapping has revitalized and redefined the traditional "block" chord-melody approach to self-accompaniment. These techniques make it physically possible to extract independent melody, harmony, and bass parts from vertical chord structures.

It is assumed that the majority of players interested in solo guitar have already had at least some acquaintance with either traditional thumb-and-finger techniques or various adaptations like pick-and-fingers or thumbpick-and-fingers. While all these techniques are applicable to the material in this book, I've chosen to use the traditional designations for the classical guitar when referring to the picking hand:

*p* = thumb, *i* = index, *m* = middle, *a* = ring finger, *c* = pinky finger

For players unfamiliar with fingerstyle technique or pick-and-finger players who would like to add thumb-and-finger technique to their palette, I've provided a brief overview of basic strokes and hand placement along with some helpful principles for choosing fingerings for the plucking hand at the end of the book. See also the Chapter 2 Guide List, which features books that specialize in a variety of fingerstyle techniques.

## Five Fingerstyle Applications for Vertical Chord Structures

1. Repetition of entire chord shape below the top melody note (R.E.)
2. Repetition of lower voices of chord shape (R.L.)
3. Simultaneous sounding of top (melody) and bottom (bass) notes of chord shape (T.B.)
4. Repetition of inner voices between top and bottom voices (R.I.)
5. Sounding of individual voices of the chord shape as in an arpeggio (Arp.)

## Preliminary Exercises for the Plucking Hand

These exercises show how we can extract melody, chords and bass parts from a vertical chord shape.

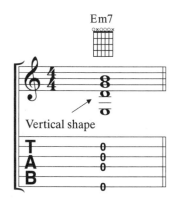

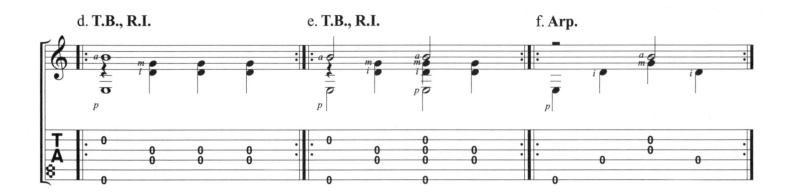

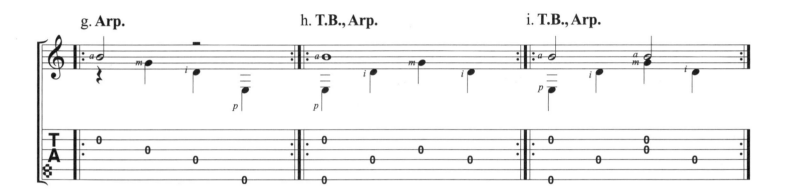

**Important note on finger placement:** When a melody note is included in the chord shape that follows, depress the entire shape first as you simultaneously play the melody and then follow with the remaining chord tone. See Example 8, measure 2 and Example 9, Measures 3 and 4.

Examples 8 – 11 are chord melody derivations based on the chord shapes employed in Chapter 1 for "The More I See You," "Alone Together," "My Funny Valentine," and "My Foolish Heart."

Please note: Each example uses the chord shapes employed in Chapter 1.

**Example 8: The More I See You (Chord-Melody Derivations)**

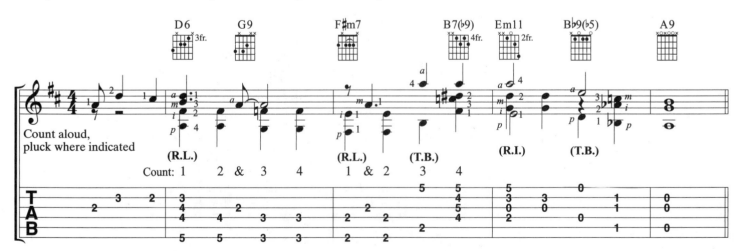

### Example 9: Alone Together (Chord-Melody Derivations)

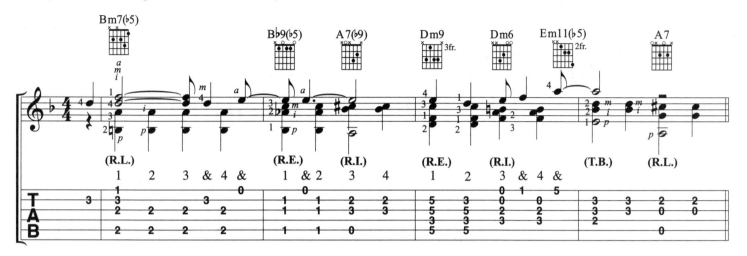

### Example 10: My Funny Valentine (Chord-Melody Derivations)

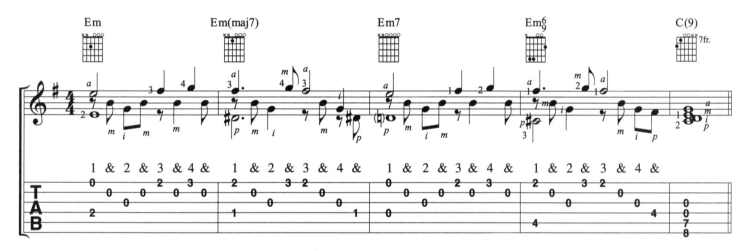

### Example 11: My Foolish Heart (Chord-Melody Derivations)

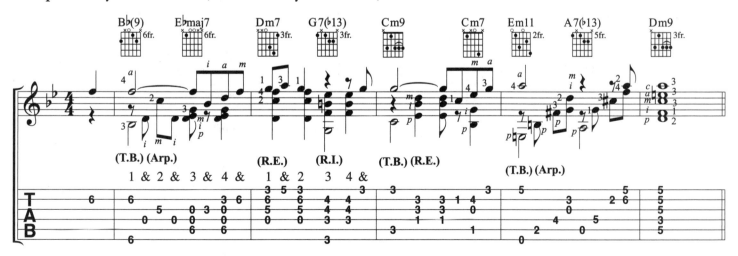

## "The More I See You," version no. 1

The moderate, steady beat for this treatment is produced by rhythmic repetition below the melody part of either the entire chord shape or lower or inner voices.

The melody part is sounded primarily with the *"a"* finger, on occasion with the *"m"* finger, and, in a five-voice chord shape, with *p, i, m, a, c*. (Five-voice chord shapes may also be sounded with a down-stroke of the thumb (*p*).) The chord and bass parts are sounded with *p, p-i, p-i-m, p-m* and *i-m*.

# THE MORE I SEE YOU
## (Version 1)

Lyrics by
MACK GORDON
Music by
HARRY WARREN
*Arranged by*
*HOWARD MORGEN*

## Guide List for Chapter 2

See the Master Guide List at the end of the book for publisher and item number information for each book.

### *Complete Jazz Guitar Method: Mastering Jazz Guitar: Chord/Melody*, Jody Fisher
Pick style, fingerstyle, pick and fingers, pages 6–7.

### *Classic Guitar Technique, Volume I*, Aaron Shearer
Fingerstyle techniques and reading.

### *The Art of Solo Guitar Book 1*, Jody Fisher
Advantages of fingerstyle for solo jazz guitar, pages 10–11.

### *Concepts: Arranging for Fingerstyle Guitar*, Howard Morgen
Developing independence between the thumb and fingers of the plucking hand, pages 7–9, 175–176, 178–184.
Adapting chord-melody style arrangements for fingerstyle, pages 106–110, "Blue Moon" page 111.

### *Fingerstyle Jazz* , Various Authors
Seventeen great jazz standards arranged for easy/intermediate-level fingerstyle guitar.

# Chapter 3:
# Comping Below a Melody Part with
# Chord Fragments and Interval Shapes

"Comping" is a style originated by jazz pianists—think of the jazz pianist's left hand as he "comps" behind his own improvised solo. Comping connotes a sparse, swinging approach to self-accompaniment that employs short, syncopated bursts of chord fragments to imply and punctuate the harmony. Comping is a particularly useful approach for jazz guitarists limited to the fingers of one fretting hand.

Most chords can be implied by two-, three-, or four-note chord fragments* provided the fragments are applied in the correct harmonic context. Performed fingerstyle or with pick-and-finger technique, using chord fragments makes it possible for the fretting hand to comp chords and bass lines while simultaneously playing melody lines.

## Chord Fragments

### Extracting Chord Fragments from "Parent" Chord Shapes

Chord fragments are derived by eliminating non-essential chord tones from larger "parent" chord structures. Most often omitted are roots and 5ths (unless specified in the chord symbol as #5 or b5), but other chord tones can also be considered non-essential, depending on the harmonic context. Your ear can often be a reliable guide when selecting which tones to omit.

### Comping with Chord Fragments

Examples 12 and 13 demonstrate the use of two- and three-note chord fragments extracted from parent chord formations. The "parent" chord shapes are placed in grids above the standard notation.

### Example 12: The More I See You (excerpt)

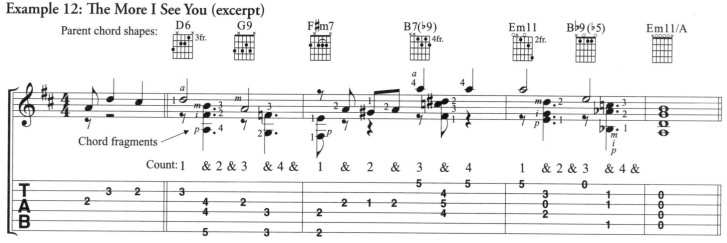

### Example 13: Alone Together (excerpt)

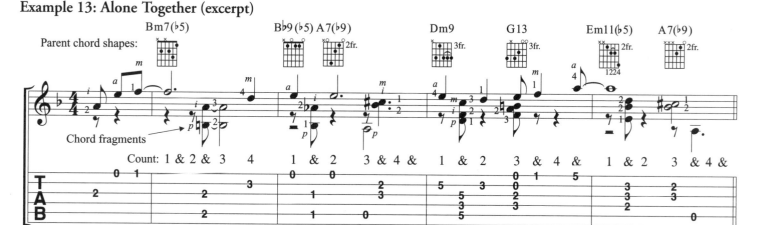

*See "Chords of Omission," Part 2, Chapter 6, page 62.

Notice how chord fragments syncopated against a melody in short, percussive bursts can create a lighter, more swinging effect than a straight chord-melody based approach. For instance, compare Example 12 to the first four measures of "The More I See You," version no. 1 (page 26) which employs the same parent chord shapes.

## Interval Shapes

### Chord Fragments as Interval Shapes

Depending on context, any interval on any set of strings can be employed as a chord fragment for comping below a melody line. The most frequently used interval shapes are the perfect 4th, the augmented 4th/diminished 5th (tritone), and the perfect 5th. See Figure 4.

**Figure 4:** String set 4-3.

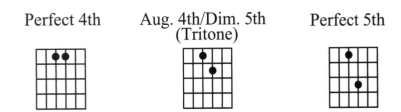

The *same* interval shape and fret location on the fingerboard can imply *different* chord letter names and qualities depending on the location of the chord root in relation to the interval shape. For example...

**Figure 5:** With the tritone shape.

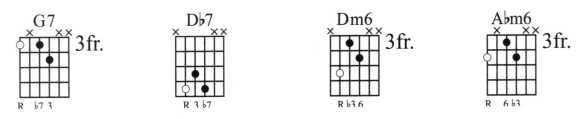

**Figure 6:** With the perfect 4th shape.

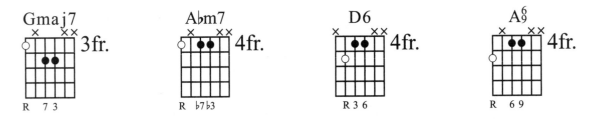

**Figure 7:** With the perfect 5th shape.

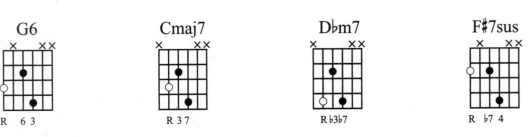

The *same* interval shape placed at neighboring fretboard locations can imply different chord qualities for one chord.

**Figure 8:** With the perfect 4th shape.

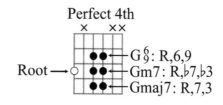

**Figure 9:** With the perfect 5th shape.

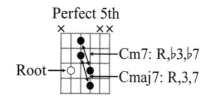

## Visualizing Interval Shape Placement

Interval shapes employed as chord fragments are most often played on string sets 4-3, 5-4 and 6-5.

### String Set 4-3

Figures 10 and 11 each show two ways to visualize the tritone shape implying G7 at the 3rd and 9th frets.

**Figure 10:** From implied roots on either the 6th or 4th strings.

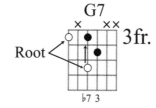

**Figure 11:** From implied roots on either the 5th or 3rd strings.

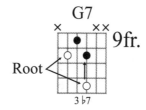

### String Set 5-4

**Figure 12:** Shows two ways to visualize the tritone shape implying D7 at the 3rd and 9th frets. At the 3rd fret, the implied root is located on the 5th string. At the 9th fret, the implied root is located either on the 6th or 4th strings.

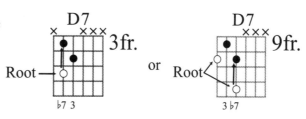

**String Set 6-5**

**Figure 13:** Shows two ways to visualize the tritone shape, implying A7 at the 3rd and 9th frets. At the 3rd fret, the implied root is located on the 6th string. At the 9th fret, the implied root is located on the 5th string.

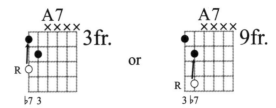

**Using Perfect 4th Shapes**

**Figure 14:** Shows how to use perfect 4th shapes to imply major 7th and minor 7th chords on string sets 4-3, 5-4, and 6-5.

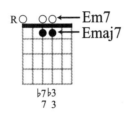
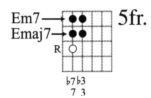
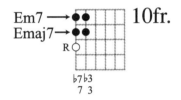

**Using Perfect 5th Shapes**

**Figure 15:** Shows how to use perfect 5th shapes to imply major 7th and minor 7th chords on string sets 4-3 and 5-4. (String set 6-5 is not practical.)

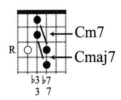
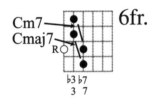

# Choosing the String Set

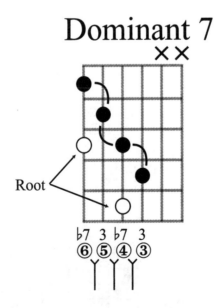

The diagram above shows three possible string sets for the tritone shape within a dominant 7th chord. Each of these shapes will be used in the following examples.

Choosing a string set is usually a matter of convenience and availability as well as the sound quality produced on different thicknesses of the strings. The only difference between the following examples (14, 14a, and 14b) is the choice of string set for the tritone shapes implying B7, E7, A7, and D7. Pluck all melody notes with the middle or ring finger (*m* or *a*) and interval shapes with thumb (*p*) and index (*i*). Each of these examples is based on a excerpt from "Nice Work If You Can Get It."

## Example 14

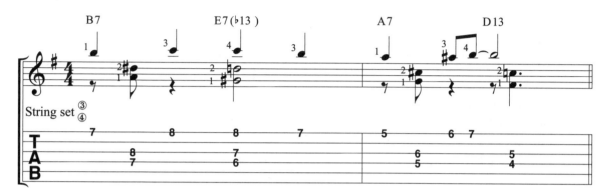

## Example 14a

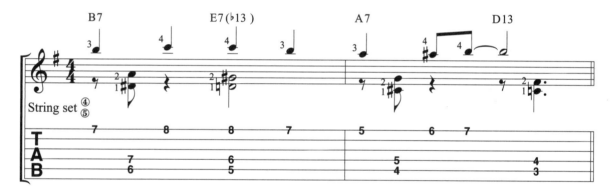

## Example 14b

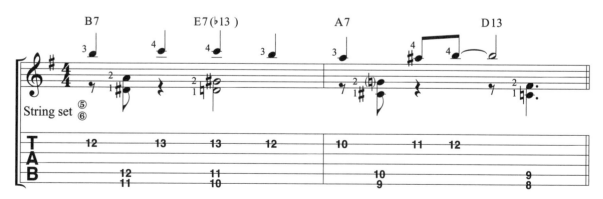

34

# Visualizing Interval Shapes Across String Sets
## Visualizing Perfect 4th and Perfect 5th Interval Shapes Across String Sets 6-5, 5-4, and 4-3
Figure 17            Figure 18

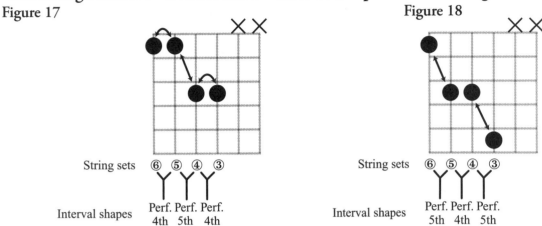

Figure 17 shows how a perfect 4th shape on string set 4-3, **when inverted**, becomes a perfect 5th shape on 5-4. Then, the perfect 5th shape on 5-4, **when inverted,** becomes a perfect 4th shape on 6-5. The perfect 4th shape on 6-5 is one octave lower in pitch than the identical perfect 4th shape on 4-3.

## Interval Shapes on 4-3, 5-4 and 6-5 Implying Em7–A7–Dmaj7–D6–Dm7–G7–Cmaj7

**Example 15**

String set 4-3:

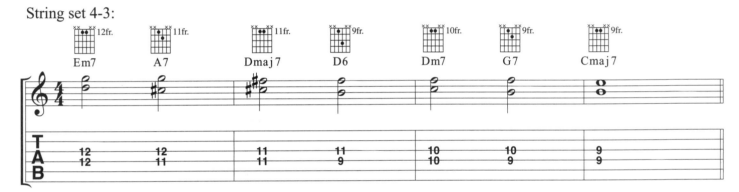

**Example 15a**

String set 5-4:

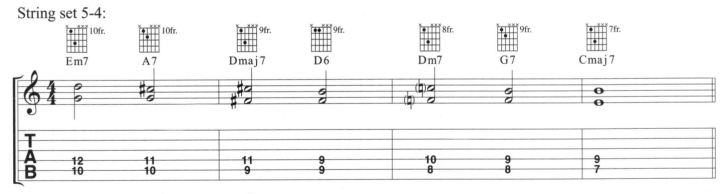

**Example 15b**

String set 6-5:

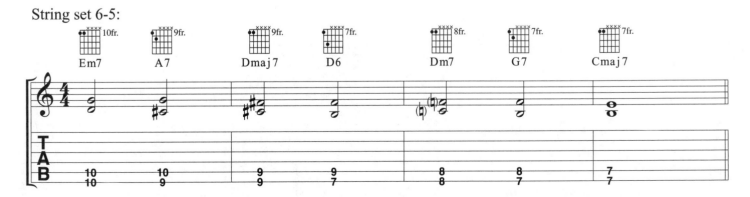

Figure 18 (see top of page 34) shows how a perfect 5<sup>th</sup> shape on string set 4-3, **when inverted**, becomes a perfect 4<sup>th</sup> shape on 5-4. Then, the perfect 4<sup>th</sup> shape on 5-4, **when inverted,** becomes a perfect 5<sup>th</sup> shape on 6-5. The perfect 5<sup>th</sup> shape on 6-5 is one octave lower in pitch than the identical perfect 5<sup>th</sup> shape on 4-3.

## Interval Shapes on 4-3, 5-4 and 6-5 Implying Am7–D7–Gmaj7–G6–Gm7–C7–Fmaj7

**Example 16**

String set 4-3:

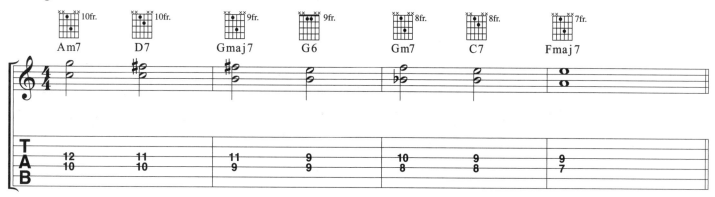

String set 5-4:

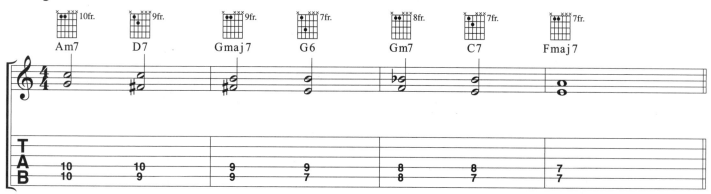

String set 6-5:

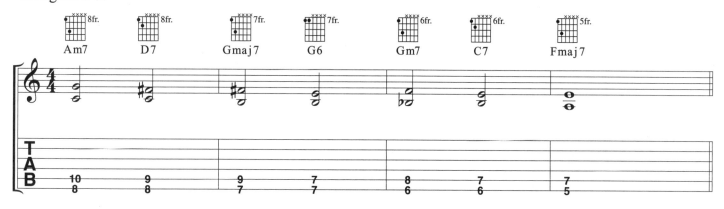

## Comping on String Sets 4-3 and 5-4 with Tritone, Perfect 4th, and Perfect 5th Shapes

The chord grids placed above the standard notation for this sixteen-bar "head" for "Speak Low" (Example 17) are visualization aids displaying both the interval shapes implying the chord progression and the location of their related chord roots on the fingerboard.

Note that any interval can be used as a chord fragment. (See the minor 3rd interval shape in the measure 6 implying A7(♭9) and the major 3rd interval shape implying B9 in measure 8.)

Example 17

# SPEAK LOW
### (excerpt)

## "Nice Work If You Can Get It"

This treatment of George and Ira Gershwin's "Nice Work If You Can Get It" features comping with the tritone interval shape, three- and four-note chord fragments, "block" chord-melody style, and chord-melody derivations. Other important elements in the arrangement include voice leading (note the descending chromatic motion of the tritone shapes implying cycle pattern B7–E7–A7–D7–G7) and a funky walking bass line at measures 34–35. Voice leading and cycle patterns are discussed at length in Part 2. The walking bass line approach is discussed and demonstrated in Chapter 5.

Following is the reasoning behind the selection of suggested fingerings for the plucking hand in measures 19, 31, and 32.

When the plucking hand is positioned over the strings, the middle finger (*m*) extends slightly lower than the index finger (*i*), and the ring finger (*a*) extends slightly lower than the middle finger (*m*). It will cause less tension in the plucking hand to maintain this natural alignment when crossing strings.

> *m* crosses ahead of *a* to the next higher string.
> *a* crosses ahead of *m* to the next higher string
> *i* crosses in back of *m* to the next lower string
> *m* crosses in back of *a* to the next lower string

Example 18 demonstrates how these principles are applied to the suggested plucking hand fingering at measure 19.

**Example 18**

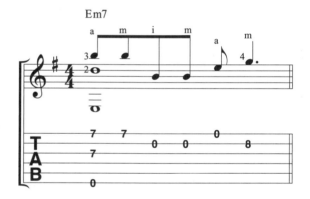

Example 19 demonstrates the use of the pinky finger (*c*) for chords at measures 31 and 32. Using "*c*" takes some practice but can be very efficient, especially when sounding five-note chords. Notice also how *p*, *i*, and *m* come into play when executing the funky bass line with a muted-string triplet effect at measures 31 and 32.

**Example 19**

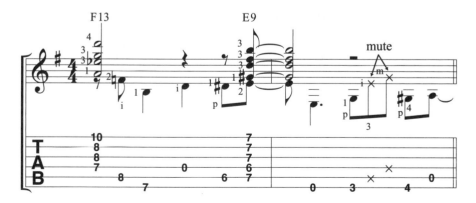

# NICE WORK IF YOU CAN GET IT

Words by
IRA GERSHWIN
Music by
GEORGE GERSHWIN
*Arranged by*
*HOWARD MORGEN*

**Moderate swing**

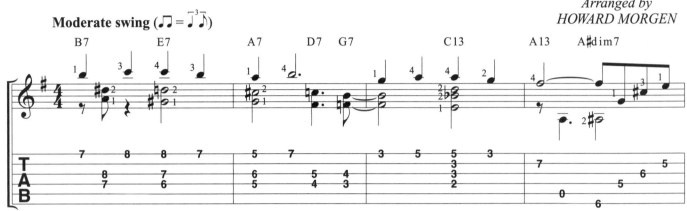

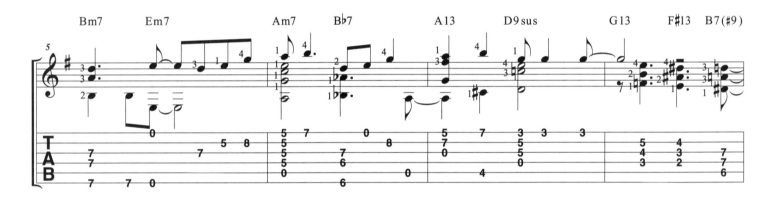

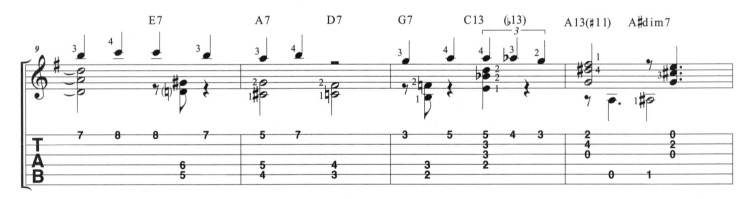

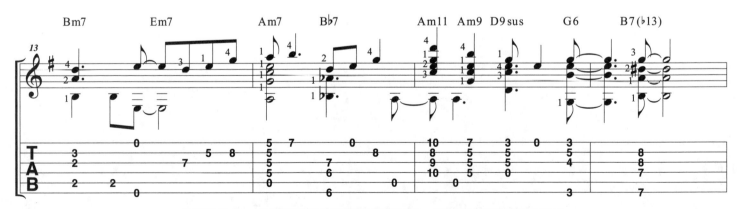

## Guide List for Chapter 3

See the Master Guide List at the end of the book for publisher and item number information for each book.

*Jazz Guitar Harmony,* **Jody Fisher**
Comping with abbreviated voicings, pages 21–22 and 35–39.

*Howard Morgen's Solo Guitar (Insights, Arranging Techniques & Classic Jazz Standards)*
Visualizing chord fragments, pages 33–39.
"In Your Own Sweet Way," pages 40–43.
"Stompin' at the Savoy," pages 44–48.

*Lenny Breau Fingerstyle Jazz*
Comping below the melody with chord fragments and interval shapes, pages 13–18.

*Chord Chemistry,* **Ted Greene**
Voicing concepts for comping with chord fragments and interval shapes, pages 105–109.

# Chapter 4:
# Sounding the Melody in the Bass,
# Below the Chord Accompaniment

This less conventional approach to self-accompaniment produces a pleasing "two guitar" effect that, once mastered, can be lots of fun to play. It requires a high level of independence between the thumb and fingers because of the natural tendency of the thumb to "go along" with the fingers. This is especially true if the melody is syncopated against a steady "four-to-the-bar" chord accompaniment.

In the excerpt from "Alone Together" in Example 20, carefully follow the fingering suggestions for both hands and check the TAB for the location of the melody part along the fingerboard. Count aloud and pluck where indicated.

**Example 20**

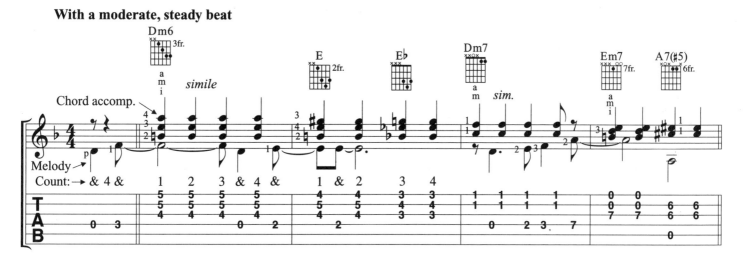

## Exercises for Developing Independence Between Thumb and Fingers

Sound all down-stemmed notes with your thumb and up-stemmed notes with your fingers. In order to maintain free, unhindered movement of the thumb and fingers, you need to hold your hand so that your thumb points out and away from your fingers. This hand position helps curb the tendency of the thumb to stray in behind the fingers. Pluck the strings lightly. The plucking motion for your fingers should originate in the second knuckle joint (where the finger joins the hand). Avoid the natural tendency to hook or snap the strings. Play through each exercise several times.

**Exercise 3a**

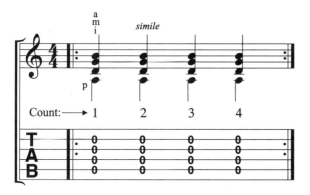

**Exercise 3b**

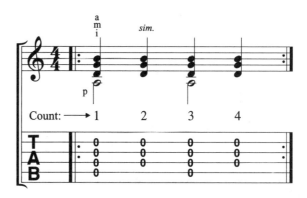

**Exercise 3c**

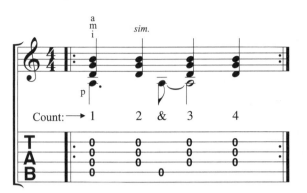

**Exercise 3d**

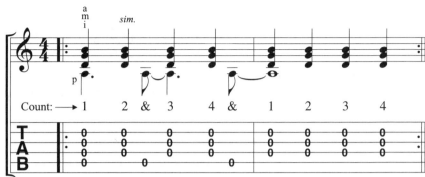

**Exercise 3e**

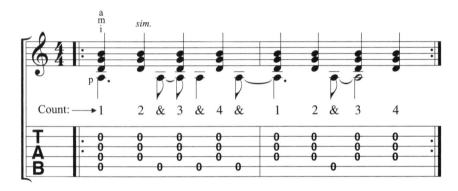

**Exercise 3f**

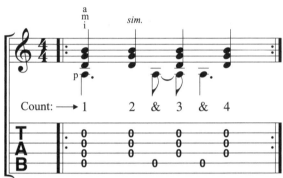

**Exercise 3g**

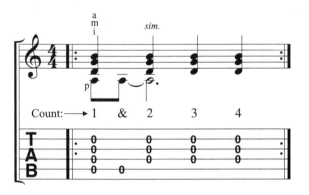

**Exercise 3h**

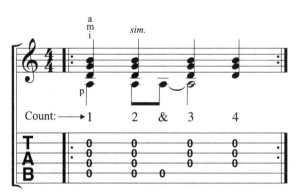

**Exercise 3i**

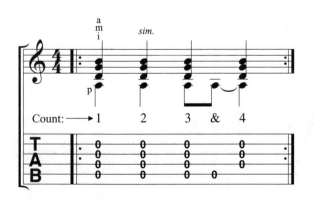

**Exercise 3j**

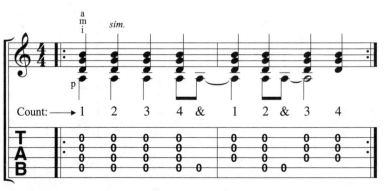

**Exercise 3k**

**Exercise 3l**

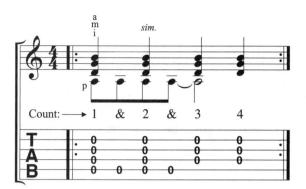

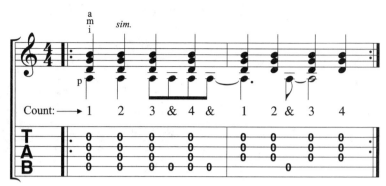

**Exercise 3m**

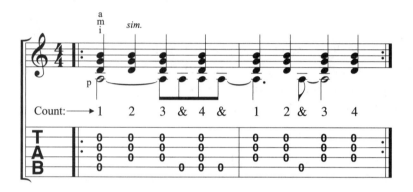

**Exercise 3n**

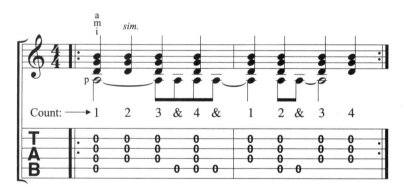

# Setting Up an Arrangement*

Step 1: Locate the melody along the lower bass strings. Keep the upper strings available for chord accompaniment. See Example 21.

**Example 21: The More I See You (excerpt, measures 1-4)**

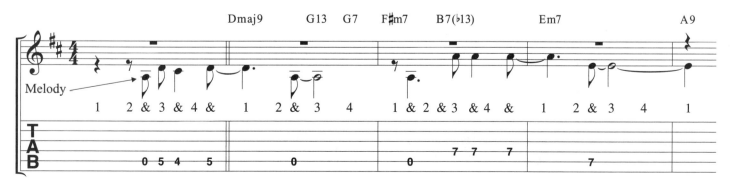

Step 2: Based on your choice of location along the bass strings for the melody, search for available chord tones on the upper strings within the span of your fretting hand.

**Example 21a: The More I See You (excerpt, with comping)**

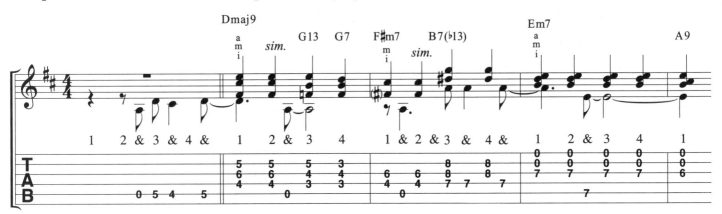

**Note:** Many chord shapes that are routinely employed for chord-melody and comping below a melody line are not available when the melody is confined to the lower bass strings. You'll need to create your own, non-garden variety, chord voicings by searching the upper strings for whatever chord tones are available within the span of your fretting hand. (See Chord Construction, Chord Voicing, Non-Garden Variety Voicings, and Chords of Omission in Part 2.)

*It's advisable to experiment with more than one location for the melody part along the bass strings before making a final commitment since your choice of location is the governing factor that will determine the availability of chord tones for your chord accompaniment.

Examples 22 and 22a demonstrate two additional possibilities for measures 3 and 4 of "The More I See You." These examples can also substitute for measures 3 and 4 in "The More I See You," version no. 2.

**Example 22: The More I See You (excerpt)**

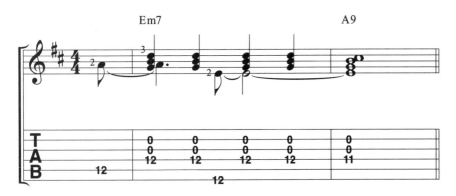

**Example 22a: With harmonics**

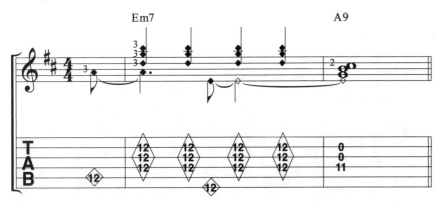

## "The More I See You," version no. 2

In conceiving this arrangement, I tried to replicate the driving rhythmic feel of my favorite jazz pianist—the great Errol Garner—with his steady, laid back, just-behind-the-beat left-hand chord accompaniment contrasted against his puckish, good-humored melodic sense.

The most challenging aspect of playing this arrangement is maintaining separation and independence between the melody and accompaniment parts. All up-stemmed chords are played with the fingers and should be sounded at a steady, even tempo in quarter notes. The thumb sounds the highly syncopated melody part on and off the beat with a "swing-eighth" feel.

Sound the chords softly by lightly plucking the strings on the tips of your fingers but with enough volume to bring out the occasional counter-melodies voiced among the chords. These counter-melodies help to give the accompaniment a life of its own. Sound all melody notes with greater volume than the accompaniment and make certain that all tied notes and open strings are sustained for their full time value.

The muting technique for the sixteenth-note and eighth-note triplet figures in measure 33 is accomplished by lightly laying the first finger of the fretting hand across 3rd, 4th, and 5th strings without depressing the strings and plucking as indicated with *i* or *p-m-i*.

# THE MORE I SEE YOU
## (Version 2)

Lyrics by
MACK GORDON
Music by
HARRY WARREN
*Arranged by*
*HOWARD MORGEN*

**Moderate, with a steady beat**

*Intro:*

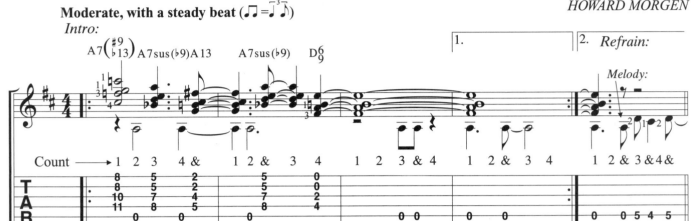

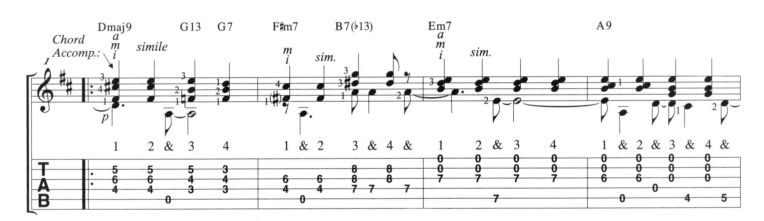

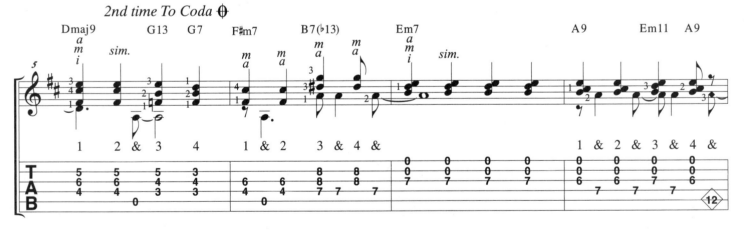

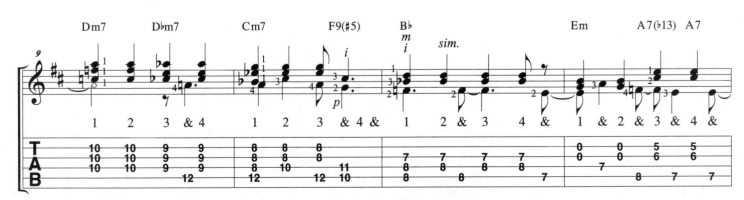

## Guide List for Chapter 4

See the Master Guide List at the end of the book for publisher and item number information for each book.

### *Serie Didactica para la Guitarra Cuaderno 2 Technica de la Mano Derecha* (English and Spanish)

Development of plucking-hand thumb technique, pages 24–32 and 41–42.

### *All Blues for Jazz Guitar, Comping Styles, Chords and Grooves,* Jim Ferguson

Playing melodic bass lines below a chord accompaniment, pages 68–86.

### *Complete Jazz Guitar Method: Mastering Jazz Guitar: Chord/Melody,* Jody Fisher

Bass lines with chord accompaniment, pages 50–57.

### *Concepts: Arranging for Fingerstyle Guitar,* Howard Morgen

Three against two, pages 116–117.

### *Lenny Breau Fingerstyle Jazz*

Three against two, pages 19–22.

# Chapter 5:
## The Walking Bass Line

Derived from chord tones, passing tones, and neighbor tones, a well-constructed walking bass line can imply an entire chord progression. Think of the times you've heard a singer or horn player backed up by a lone bass player. When used in conjunction with other approaches to self-accompaniment, walking bass lines contribute continuity, melodic counterpoint, and rhythmic drive to the mix. A typical walking bass line is comprised of ascending and descending stepwise and intervallic melodic motion, abrupt changes of direction, and syncopation.

**Example 23**

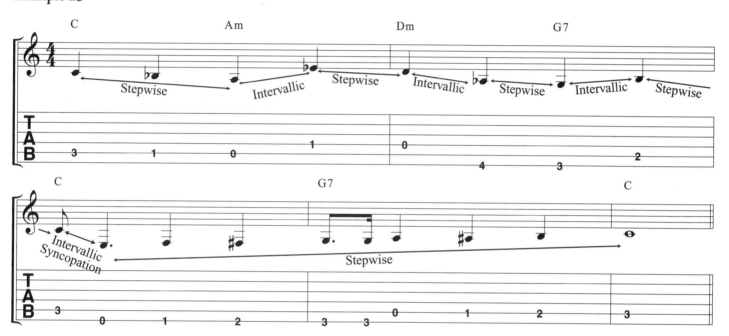

## Components of a Walking Bass Line

The following examples are based on a G major scale.

**Figure 19**

Chord Tones (CT): Notes that belong to the chord as indicated by the chord symbol.

**Figure 19a**

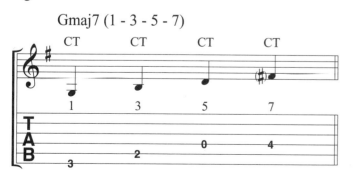

Passing Tones (PT): Notes that lie between chord tones; may be diatonic (DPT) or chromatic (ChPT). Diatonic passing tones belong to the scale of the given chord.

**Figure 19b**

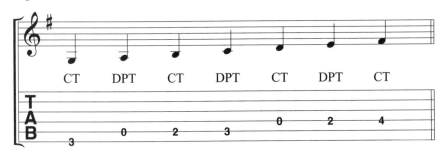

Chromatic passing tones are non-scale tones that lie between diatonic tones.

**Figure 19c**

Upper and Lower Neighbor Tones (UN, LN): An upper neighbor tone may be either a passing tone or a chord tone. To be considered an upper neighbor, it must resolve either a whole or a half step down to its neighboring chord tone.

**Example 19d:**

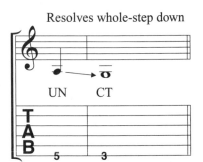

A lower neighbor tone can be either a passing tone or a chord tone. To be considered a lower neighbor it must resolve up a half step to its neighboring chord tone.

**Figure 19e**

# How Chord Tones, Passing Tones, and Neighbor Tones Function in a Walking Bass Line

Example 24 illustrates the application and function of chord tones, passing tones, and neighbor tones in the following chord progression.

| Progression: | C | Am | /Dm | G7 | /C | G7 | /C |
|---|---|---|---|---|---|---|---|
| Chord Tones: | C-E-G | A-C-E | D-F-A | G-B-D-F | C-E-G | G-B-D-F | C-E-G |

**Example 24**

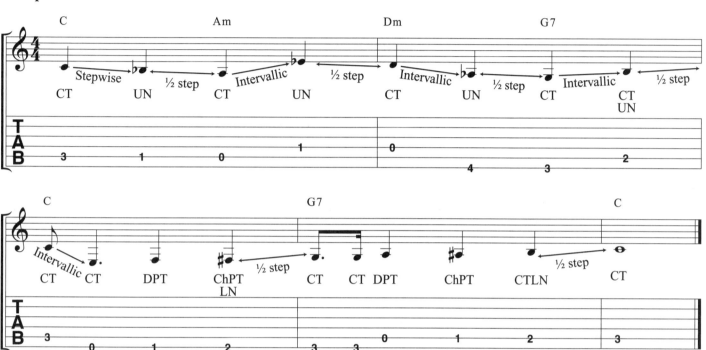

Notice in the above example how neighbor tones placed on the beat before a chord help to create a smooth transition from one chord to the next.

The following exercise shows how to use your plucking-hand fingers on a walking bass line implying a I–vi–ii–V7 progression in G major. Sound the majority of quarter notes in this exercise with your thumb (*p*). Sound the eighth-note triplet figure in measure 3 and the dotted eighth- and sixteenth-note figures in measures 1 and 4 as indicated with *p* and *i*.

**Exercise 4**

# Four Suggestions for Building Melodically Interesting Walking Bass Lines

1. Use stepwise diatonic and/or chromatic motion in conjunction with intervallic leaps and abrupt changes of direction (Example 25, measures 1–4).

2. Place chord tones on the beat and passing tones on the off beat (Example 25, measure 2).

3. Place upper and/or lower neighbor tones on the beat before a chord change (Example 25, measures 1–3).

4. Syncopate your bass line by placing accents both on and off the beat with ties, dotted notes, and triplets (Example 26, measure 2).

**Example 25**

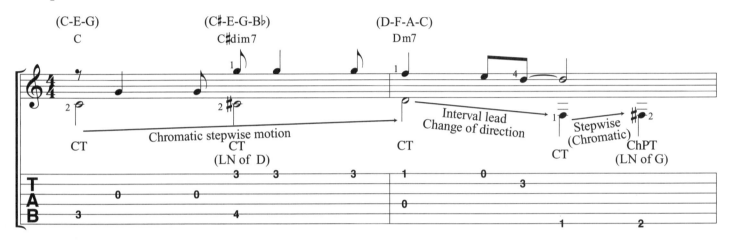

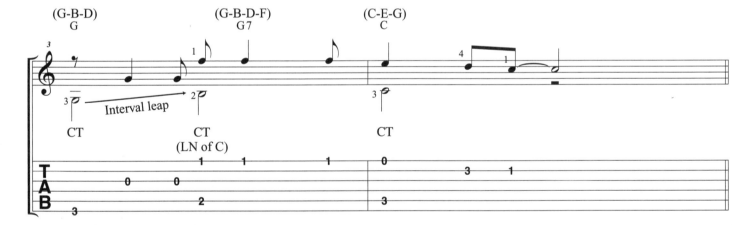

**Example 26**

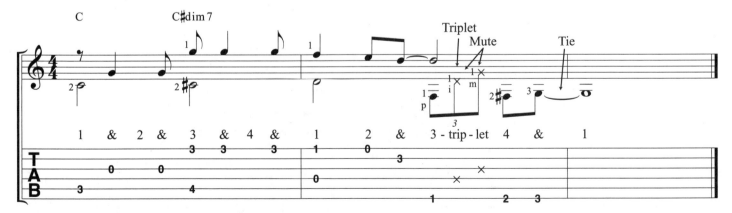

It's rare that walking bass lines are employed exclusively throughout an entire arrangement. In practice, most solo jazz arrangements including walking bass lines are fleshed out with chords and often contain many, if not all, the approaches to self-accompaniment featured in Part 1.

**Example 27**

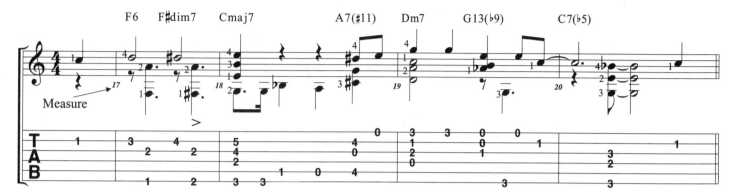

Exercise 5 is a "hands-on" introduction to building a walking bass line below a melody with chord, passing tones, and neighbor tones.

On the next page is a worksheet supplying the melody, chord progression and chord spellings (see Figure 20) for "It's Only a Paper Moon" written in standard notation and TAB. Below the accompaniment are the following hints to help you stay on course as you fill in the walking bass line where indicated.

1. Strategically located "landmark" bass notes that indicate the general direction for the bass line.

2. Symbols designating chord tones (CT), diatonic and chromatic passing tones (DPT and ChPT) and neighbor tones (UN, LN).

3. TAB suggesting possible string and fret locations for the bass line.

In order to avoid possible conflicts between the melody and bass parts, always sing, hum, or whistle the melody while experimenting with potential walking bass lines. When completed, compare your results with "It's Only a Paper Moon," version no. 1 on page 56.

**Figure 20**

| Chord | Chord Tones | | | | |
|---|---|---|---|---|---|
| C | C | E | G | | |
| C#dim7 | C# | E | G | B♭ | |
| Dm7 | D | F | A | C | |
| G | G | B | D | | |
| F | F | A | C | | |
| D7 | D | F# | A | C | |
| C7(♭5) | C | E | G♭ | B♭ | |
| F6 | F | A | C | D | |
| F#dim7 | F# | A | C | E♭ | |
| B♭13 | B♭ | D | F | A♭ | G |

Exercise 5

# IT'S ONLY A PAPER MOON
(Worksheet)

*Available as a printable PDF on the enhanced CD

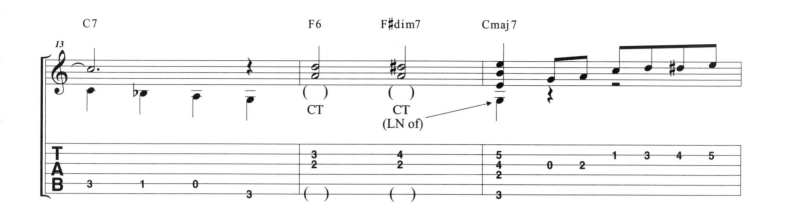

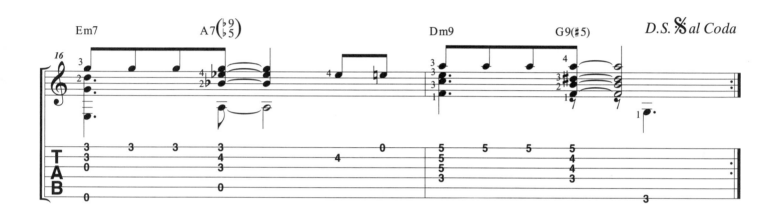

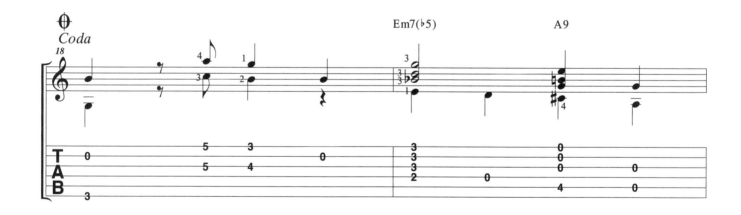

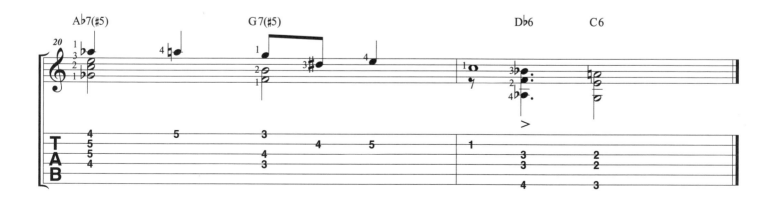

# IT'S ONLY A PAPER MOON
## (Version 1)

Words by
BILLY ROSE and E.Y. HARBURG
Music by
HAROLD ARLEN
*Arranged by*
*HOWARD MORGEN*

**Medium swing**

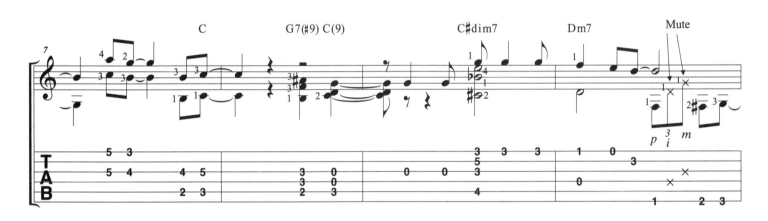

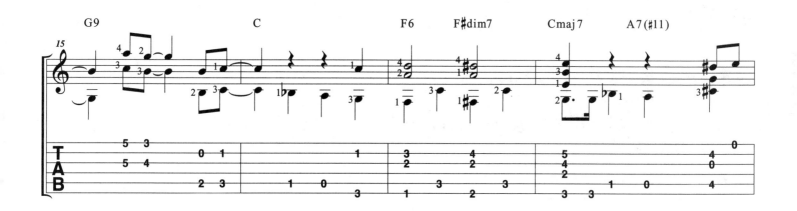

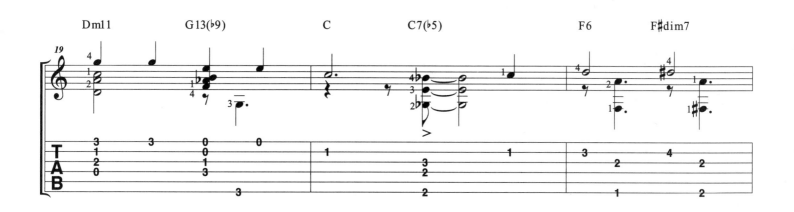

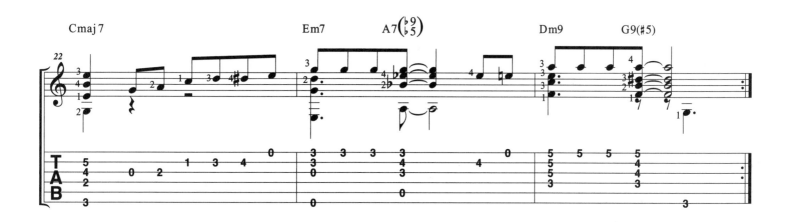

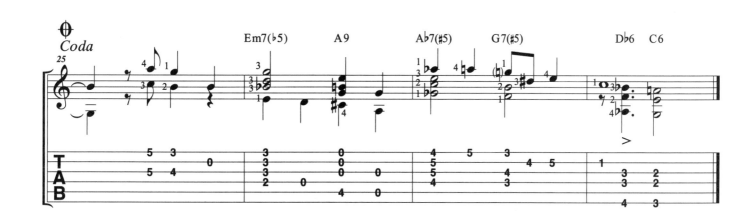

## Guide List for Chapter 5

See the Master Guide List at the end of the book for publisher and item number information
for each book.

*Teaching Your Guitar to Walk,* **Paul Musso**
Introducing the walking bass line concept.

*Jazz Guitar for Classical Cats: Chord/Melody,* **Andrew York**
"Blues for J.D.," pages 60–61.

*The Art of Solo Jazz Guitar, Book 2,* **Jody Fisher**
Comping chords with walking bass lines, pages 70–79.

*Concepts: Arranging for Fingerstyle Guitar,* **Howard Morgen**
Preparatory exercises for developing "mental" independence between two completely independent parts;
"C Jam Blues in E major," pages 31–33; "Just Friends," pages 10–11; "Sweet and Lovely," pages 96–97;
"Blues for Hy," pages 104–105.

*Intros and Endings,* **Ron Eschete**
Useful hip material that utilizes all the approaches to self-accompanied jazz guitar demonstrated in Part 1.

*Jazz Guitar Standards: Chord Melody Solos*
44 classic jazz standards.

*Fingerstyle Guitar Standards,* **Bill Piburn**
15 Classic Songs for Guitar Solo

*Fingerstyle Love Songs,* **Bill Piburn**
15 Classic Songs Arranged for Solo Guitar

*Jimmy Wyble's Solo Collection,* Jimmy Wyble

*Concepts for the Classical and Jazz Guitar,* Jimmy Wyble and Ron Berman

*George Van Eps Guitar Solos (with TAB),* George Van Eps

# PART 2:

# Theoretical Information, Harmonic Concepts, Thought Processes, and Techniques

# Chapter 6:
# Terminology

## Chord Construction

All chords are built from scales. "Chord construction" refers to the patterns or numerical formulas that are applied to a major scale to spell out the chord tones for any given chord. Chord formulas are always spelled in ascending sequence from the root (the letter name of the chord). For example, the formula for constructing a major triad is R (root)–3–5, which represents the root, the third, and the fifth tones of the major scale. The formula for a minor triad is R–♭3–5, for the augmented triad is R–3–♯5 and for the diminished triad, R–♭3–♭5.

See Example 28.

**Example 28: G Major Scale**

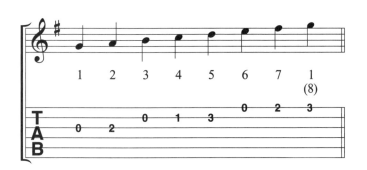
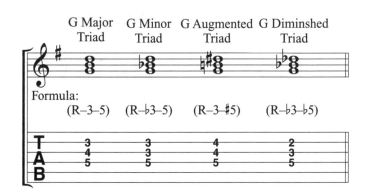

## Chord Embellishment

Like adding spice to food or color to a pencil sketch, embellishment adds color and tension to a basic chord structure with the addition of:

    1. Scale tones below the octave from the major scale of the chord root (6th and 7th):

**Example 29: A major scale**

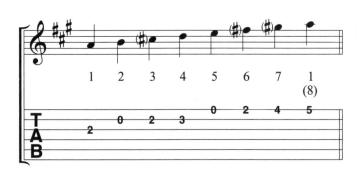

**Example 29a**

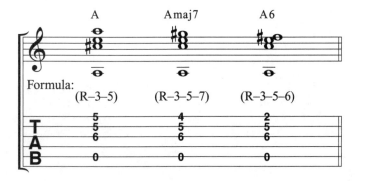

**Example 29b**

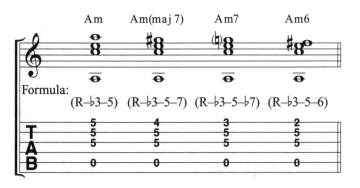

2. Diatonic Extensions: Scale tones from the major scale of the chord root extended beyond the seventh degree into the second octave (9–11–13):

**Example 30**

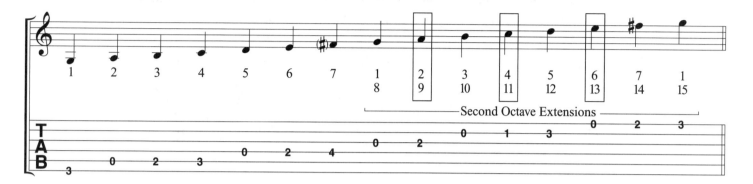

Unlike chord construction formulas, chord tones may be stacked (voiced) in any sequence:

**Example 30a**

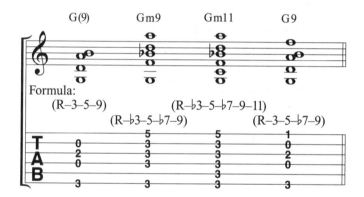

3. Chromatic Alterations: Scale tones that have been chromatically altered (usually ♯5, ♭5, ♯9, ♭9):

**Example 30b**

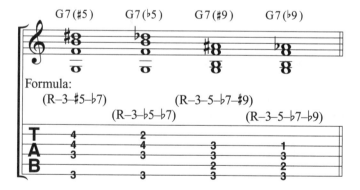

**Note:** There are only three basic chord qualities (also called "families" or "types"): Major, Minor, and Dominant 7th (diminished and augmented chords are considered subdivisions of the dominant quality). All three of these chord qualities can be embellished with scale extensions (9ths, 11ths, and 13ths) and/or alterations (♭5, ♯5, ♭9, ♯9) without changing their function within the chord progression. For example, C7(♯9), C7(♭9), C7(♯5), C7(♭5), C13, C9, C13(♭9) are all basically C7 chords with added color tones. Cmaj9, Cmaj7, C(add9), Cmaj13 and C6 all function as C major chords. Cm7, Cm9, Cm11 and Cm(maj7) all function as C minor chords.

## Chord Voicing

Chords are comprised of vertically stacked chord tones called "voices." "Chord voicing" refers to the specific order and placement of each chord tone (voice) within the chord structure. Unlike chord construction formulas, which are always spelled in consecutive, ascending order from the root, a chord voicing can be stacked in any desired sequence. See previous Examples 30a and 30b.

## Voice Leading

"Voice leading" refers to the manner in which individual tones within a chord structure approach and resolve to the tones of the following chord. In general, tones that are in common remain constant while the remaining tones move smoothly in stepwise, linear fashion from one chord to the next. The application of voice leading principles is examined in Chapters 7 and 8.

## Chords of Omission

As demonstrated in Part 1, Chapter 3, p. 29, (Extracting Chord Fragments from "parent" chord shapes), it's neither necessary, nor even desirable, to include all the possible chord tones within a chord to create a chord voicing that will imply the chord sound you want. The most often omitted notes are roots and 5ths (unless the 5th is specified in the chord symbol as ♯5 or ♭5). Extensions 9, 11, and 13 can be omitted without changing the basic chord sound or function within the progression depending upon the harmonic context. Typically, 3rds and 7ths are viewed as the most important chord tones required to imply the correct sound and for good voice leading. Decisions of which tones to omit will often depend on practical fingering considerations, the proximity of available chord tones, harmonic context, and textural preferences.

Example 31 contains some examples of major, minor, and dominant extensions with omitted chord tones.

**Example 31**

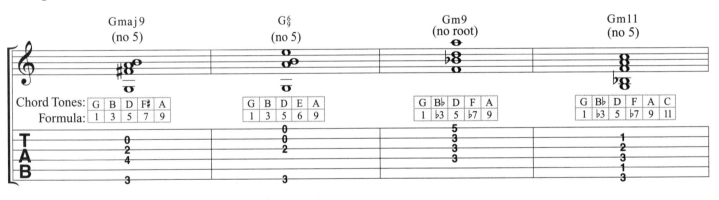

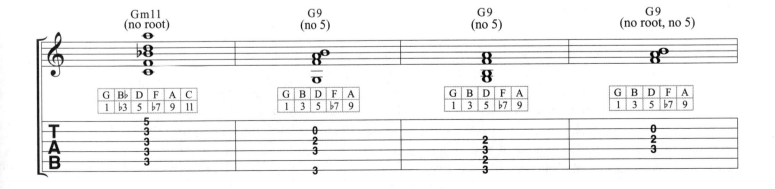

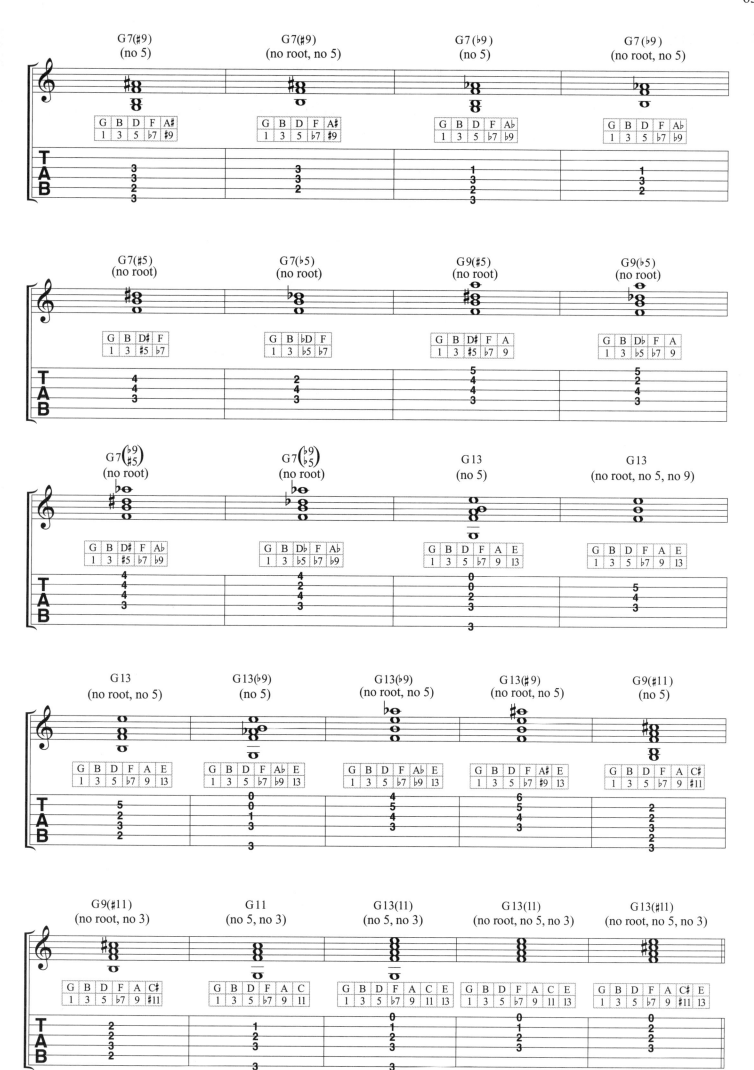

# Chord Inversion

Chords voiced with the root (R) in the bass are said to be in **root position.** When the bass note is other than the root, the chord is **inverted.** Chords voiced with the 3rd in the bass are in **first inversion.** Chords with the 5th in the bass are in **second inversion.** Chords with the 7th in the bass are in **third inversion.**

All triads have a root position and two inversions. See Figure 21.

**Figure 21:** G Major Triad, root position and two inversions.

| Formula: | R | 3 | 5 |
|---|---|---|---|
| Chord Tones: | G | B | D |

| Root Position (Root in Bass) | |
|---|---|
| 5 | D |
| 3 | B |
| R | G |

| First Inversion (3rd in bass) | |
|---|---|
| R | G |
| 5 | D |
| 3 | B |

| Second Inversion (5th in bass) | |
|---|---|
| 3 | B |
| R | G |
| 5 | D |

All seventh chords have a root position and three inversions. See Figure 21A.

**Figure 21a:** G7, root position and three inversions.

| Formula: | R | 3 | 5 | ♭7 |
|---|---|---|---|---|
| Chord Tones: | G | B | D | F |

| Root Position (Root in Bass) | |
|---|---|
| ♭7 | F |
| 5 | D |
| 3 | B |
| R | G |

| First Inversion (3rd in Bass) | |
|---|---|
| R | G |
| ♭7 | F |
| 5 | D |
| 3 | B |

| Second Inversion (5th in Bass) | |
|---|---|
| 3 | B |
| R | G |
| ♭7 | F |
| 5 | D |

| Third Inversion (7th in Bass) | |
|---|---|
| 5 | D |
| 3 | B |
| R | G |
| ♭7 | F |

The bass note always determines how the chord voicing is named regardless of how the remaining tones in the chord voicing are stacked above the bass note. See Figure 21b.

**Figure 21b:** The following are all first inversion chords, but each is "voiced" (stacked) differently.

| R | R | 5 | 5 | ♭7 | ♭7 |
|---|---|---|---|---|---|
| ♭7 | 5 | ♭7 | R | 5 | R |
| 5 | ♭7 | R | ♭7 | R | 5 |
| 3 | 3 | 3 | 3 | 3 | 3 |

Closed Voicing: A chord with all its chord tones stacked consecutively in the closest possible order within one octave. See Figure 22.

**Figure 22:** Closed voicing of Amaj7 with G♯ on top.

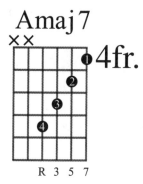

Open voicing: A chord stacked with at least one of its chord tones out of consecutive order and extending beyond one octave. See Figure 22a.

**Figure 22a:** Three open voicings of Amaj7 with G♯ on top.

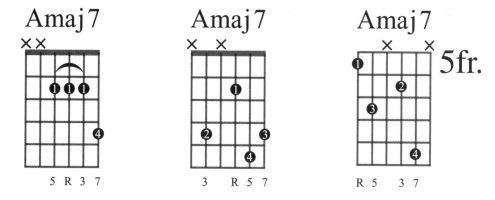

Most four-note closed voicings are accessible on guitar in root position but become difficult, if not impossible, to play when inverted because of the wide stretches dictated by the standard tuning system. There are, however, a number of very accessible open voicings that can support any given melody note. (The process of locating and applying these open voicings is demonstrated in Chapter 7.)

Example 32 illustrates three practical and accessible open voicings that replace a beautiful but difficult to play C6 chord voicing in first inversion.

**Example 32:** Four voicings for C6 with "C" on top.

C6 = C - E - G - A
   (R) (3) (5) (6)

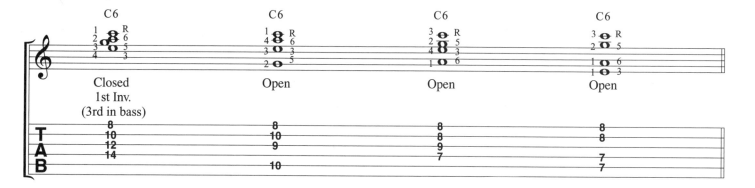

Example 33 employs open voicings for the first nine measures of "Speak Low." Notice that most of the open voicings in this example omit either the root or the 5th.

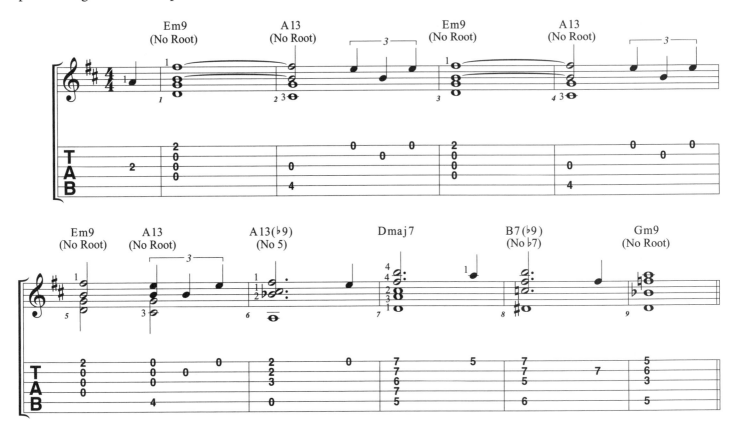

Difficult to play inversions of four-note closed voicings (Example 34) can be made accessible by simply omitting the lowest chord tone and playing as three-note closed voicings (Example 35).

### Example 34

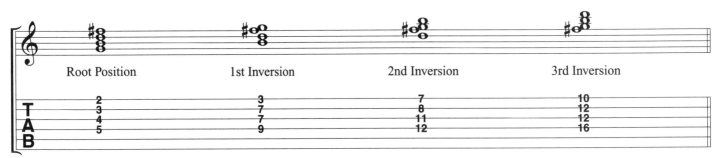

### Example 35

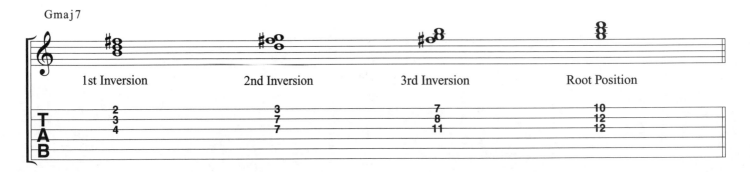

Three- and four-note closed voicings can also be both effective and accessible when employed as inversions of extended and altered chords (more on this in Chapter 7).

See Example 36—the first nine measures of "Speak Low" with closed voicings.

**Example 36: Speak Low (excerpt)**

# "Speak Low," version no. 1

A syncopated counter-melody in the bass voice lends a Latin flavor to this chord-melody treatment of "Speak Low." Chord grids are used indicate the parent chord shapes from which the two- and three-part arrangement is derived (see Part 1, Chapter 2, Chord Melody Derivations).

The majority of chord shapes are open voiced "chords of omission" labeled as: no root, no 5, no 3, etc. Fifteen of the 61 measures are voiced in root position. The remaining measures contain chords voiced in all three inversions.

In measures 33–34 of the coda, the samba inspired chord syncopations in perfect 4th intervals are played entirely with the thumb. A count is provided below the notation and above the TAB to help with the syncopations. Count aloud as you play and pluck where indicated.

# SPEAK LOW
## (Version 1)

Words by OGDEN NASH
Music by KURT WEILL

*Arranged by*
*HOWARD MORGEN*

# Guide List for Chapter 6

See the Master Guide List at the end of the book for publisher and item number information for each book.

*Creative Chord Substitution for Jazz Guitar,* **Eddie Arkin**
Well-defined essential terminology, pages 8–11.

*The Art of Solo Guitar Book 1,* **Jody Fisher**
Basic theory, pages 15–22.
Diatonic harmony, chord scales, triads, and seventh chords, pages 28–33, 39–42.
Chord construction formulas, chord families, extensions, and alterations, pages 75–80, 86–91.

*Chord Chemistry,* **Ted Greene**
Chord formulas and families, pages 9–11.

*Jazz Guitar for Classical Cats: Chord/Melody,* **Andrew York**
Triads, open and closed voicings, and passing chords, pages 6–17, 29–32.

*All Intros and Endings for Jazz Guitar*
Voice leading, pages 8–15.

*Complete Jazz Guitar Method: Mastering Jazz Guitar: Chord/Melody,* **Jody Fisher**
Voice leading, pages 22–23.

# Chapter 7:
# Chord Voicing Formulas and Insights

An extensive vocabulary of chord voicings that "work" in most situations is essential for improvising, but relying *exclusively* on garden-variety chord shapes when arranging for solo guitar can tend to limit your choices as well as your creativity. It's worth the added time and effort it may take to search for voicings *in context* that, while satisfying the harmony, can also best accommodate the direction and flow of an inner voice or bass line.

Depending on the location of any melody note on the fingerboard, there are usually a number of ways a chord supporting that note can be voiced within the span of your fretting hand. Knowledge of chord voicing formulas *in conjunction with their corresponding string sets* can shorten the process of searching for, locating and applying the needed chord tones.

## Four Chord Voicing Formulas with Corresponding String Sets

Closed, Drop 2, Drop 3, Drop 2 and 4.

### Closed Voicing Formula

In chord-melody style, closed voicings are always voiced from the top (melody) note down in the *exact descending order of chord tones derived from the chord construction formula (in thirds)*. See Figure 23.

**Figure 23:** Closed Voicing Formula.

Major 7:    R–3–5–7
Gmaj7:    G–B–D–F♯

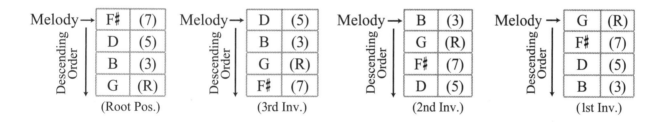

### Related String Set Configurations

*All closed voicings are located on adjacent strings.* Four-note closed voicings are located on four adjacent strings. There are three available sets of four adjacent strings on guitar:

**Figure 23a**

First set: Strings 4–3–2–1
Second set: Strings 5–4–3–2
Third Set: Strings 6–5–4–3

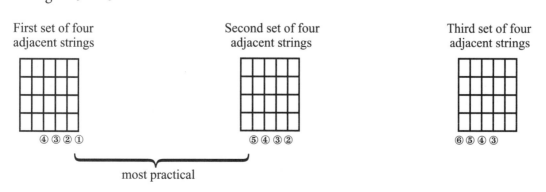

Three-note closed voicings are located on three adjacent strings. There are four available sets of three adjacent strings on guitar.

**Figure 23b**

First set:    Strings 3–2–1
Second set:   Strings 4–3–2
Third set:    Strings 5–4–3
Fourth set:   Strings 6–5–4

First set of three
adjacent strings

Second set of three
adjacent strings

Third set of three
adjacent strings

Fourth set of three
adjacent strings

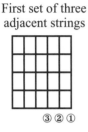

③ ② ①

④ ③ ②

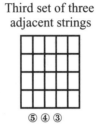

⑤ ④ ③

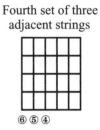

⑥ ⑤ ④

**Locating Chord Tones for Gmaj7**

**Figure 24:** Closed Voicing Formula for Gmaj7: G–B–D–F♯
1–3–5–7

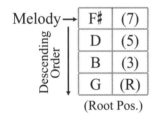

Following, in Figures 24a and 24c, are two examples of closed voicing for Gmaj7 with melody note F♯ on top. On the first set of four adjacent strings locate the chord tones in exact descending order from the melody note (F♯).

**Figure 24a**

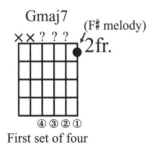

Gmaj7      (F♯ melody)

First set of four

**Procedure:** The next note after melody note F♯, in descending order, is D located on the 2nd string, followed by B on the 3rd string, followed by G on the 4th string. See Figure 24b for the solution.

**Figure 24b**

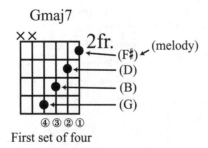

Gmaj7

First set of four

Now try the same thing only using the melody note F♯ located on 2nd string, 7th fret. This will use the second set of four adjacent strings.

**Figure 24c**

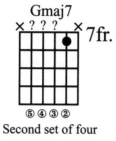

Second set of four

**Procedure:** The same approach as in Figure 24b produces D on the 3rd string, followed by B on the 4th string and G on the 5th string. See Figure 24d for the solution.

**Figure 24d**

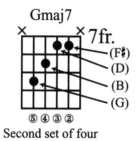

Second set of four

# Open Voicing Formulas

## The Role of Closed Voicings in the Formation of Open Voicings

The order of chord tones within any four-note closed voicing, *playable or not,* can be re-arranged so as to provide highly accessible alternative open voicings for the same melody note! The names for these voicing formulas (Drop 2, Drop 3, and Drop 2 and 4), literally describe the processes for re-arranging these tones.

*Be sure to associate each of the following chord voicing formulas with its corresponding string configuration and available string set.*

### The Drop 2 Formula

Lowering (dropping one octave) the second note from the top of any four-note closed voicing produces an open voicing that occupies four adjacent strings (see Figure 25). The Drop 2 configuration is available on three sets of four adjacent strings (see Figure 25a).

**Figure 25:** Re-arranging a closed voicing to Drop 2 open voicing.

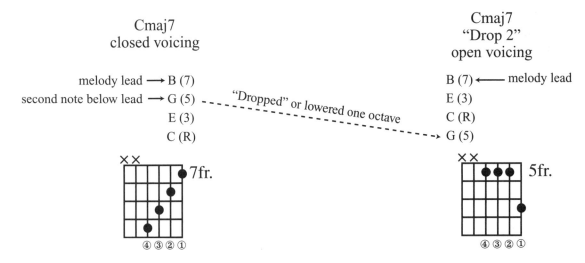

**Figure 25a:** Drop 2 voicings for Cmaj7 on three sets of four adjacent strings.

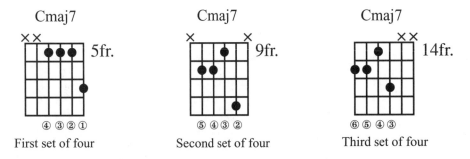

**Note:** Your choice of string sets will always depend on the string and fret location of the original melody note.

## The Drop 3 Formula

Lowering (dropping one octave) the third note from the top of any four-note closed voicing produces an open voicing that covers a five-string span—three adjacent strings with one muted string (skipped) separating the three upper voices from the lowest voice (see Figure 26). The Drop 3 configuration is available on two string sets (see Figure 26a).

**Figure 26:** Drop 3 open voicing (using Cmaj7 to illustrate).

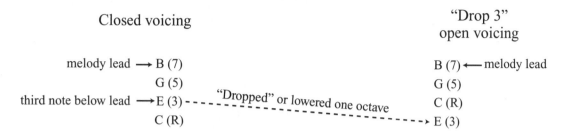

As stated before, the Drop 3 voicing will produce an open voicing that covers a five-string span with three adjacent strings on top separated from the lowest voice by one muted string. This voicing can be played on two possible strings sets:

First Set: Strings 1–2–3–5 (4th string is skipped)
Second Set: Strings 2–3–4–6 (5th string skipped)

**Figure 26a:** String configuration.

First String Set
Cmaj7

Second String Set
Cmaj7

Note: Your choice of string set will always depend on the string and fret location of the original melody note.

## The Drop 2 and 4 Formula

Lowering, by one octave, both the second and fourth notes below the top melody note of any four-note closed voicing produces an open voicing with a muted string separating two adjacent upper strings from two adjacent lower strings (see Figure 27). The Drop 2 and 4 configuration is available on two string sets.

**Figure 27:** Drop 2 and 4 open voicing (using Cmaj7 to illustrate).

As stated previously, a muted (skipped) string separates the two upper strings from the two lower strings, in a Drop 2 and 4 voicing.

First Set: Strings 1–2–4–5 (3rd string is skipped)
Second Set: Strings 2–3–5–6 (4th string skipped)

**Figure 27a:** String configuration.

First String Set

Second String Set

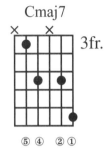

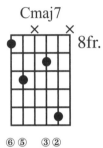

Note: Your choice of string set will always depend on the string and fret location of the original melody note.

# Chord Voicing Worksheets*

# Worksheet 1, Exercise 6

## Layout

- Column 1: Indicates the four note closed voicings for A7 in root position (Exercise 6a), first inversion (Exercise 6b), second inversion (Exercise 6c) and third inversion (Exercise 6d).

- Columns 2, 3, and 4: Indicate the Drop 2, Drop 3, and Drop 2 and 4 voicing formulas for deriving open voiced chord shapes from the parent closed chord voicings in Column 1 while *maintaining common melody note voiced on top.*

## Procedure

- Step 1: Write in chord tones in the spaces provided next to the designated string locations (only available string sets for these melody notes are indicated). The sequence of descending chord tones for each voicing is determined by applying the chord formula above each column heading to its common "parent" closed voicing in Column 1.

- Step 2: After completing the written portion of the worksheet, search for and locate each of the chord tones along its designated string and sound the resulting chord shape. Play the chord shape.

**Figure 28:** A completed sample for Exercise 6a from Worksheet 1.

| A Completed Sample for Worksheet 1, Ex. 6A Exercise 6 (Using A7 to Illustrate) | | | | | | | | | | | | | |
|---|---|---|---|---|---|---|---|---|---|---|---|---|---|
| Exercise | Column 1 | | Column 2 | | | | Column 3 | | | | Column 4 | | |
| 6A: Root Position (Melody note is G.) | "Parent" four-note closed voicing | | Drop 2: Lower second note from top by one octave | | | | Drop 3: Lower third note from top | | | | Drop 2 and 4: Lower second and fourth notes | | |
| | Formula | A7 | Notes | String Set | | | Notes | String Set | | | Notes | String Set | | |
| | (♭7) | G | G | 1 | 2 | 3 | G | 1 | 2 | | G | 1 | 2 | |
| | (5) | E | (C♯) | 2 | 3 | 4 | (E) | 2 | 3 | | (C♯) | 2 | 3 | |
| | (3) | C♯ | (A) | 3 | 4 | 5 | (A) | 3 | 4 | | (E) | 4 | 5 | |
| | (R) | A | (E) | 4 | 5 | 6 | (C♯) | 4 | 5 | | (A) | 5 | 6 | |

* *Chord voicing worksheets 1–3 are available as printable PDFs on the enhanced CD.*

# Worksheet 1
## Exercise 6 (Using A7 to Illustrate)

|  | Column 1 | Column 2 | Column 3 | Column 4 |
|---|---|---|---|---|

### 6A: Root Position (Melody note is G)

| Column 1: "Parent" 4-note closed voicing | | Column 2: Drop 2: Lower 2nd note from top by one octave | | Column 3: Drop 3: Lower 3rd note from top | | Column 4: Drop 2 and 4: Lower 2nd and 4th notes | |
|---|---|---|---|---|---|---|---|
| Formula | A7 | Notes | String Set | Notes | String Set | Notes | String Set |
| (♭7) | G | G | 1 2 3 | G | 1 2 | G | 1 2 |
| (5) | E | ( ) | 2 3 4 | ( ) | 2 3 | ( ) | 2 3 |
| (3) | C♯ | ( ) | 3 4 5 | ( ) | 3 4 | ( ) | 4 5 |
| (R) | A | ( ) | 4 5 6 | ( ) | 4 5 | ( ) | 5 6 |

### 6B: 1st Inversion (Melody note is A)

| "Parent" Chord | | Drop 2 | | Drop 3 | | Drop 2 and 4 | |
|---|---|---|---|---|---|---|---|
| Formula | A7 | Notes | String Set | Notes | String Set | Notes | String Set |
| (R) | A | A | 1 2 3 | A | 1 2 | A | 1 2 |
| (♭7) | G | ( ) | 2 3 4 | ( ) | 2 3 | ( ) | 2 3 |
| (5) | E | ( ) | 3 4 5 | ( ) | 3 4 | ( ) | 4 5 |
| (3) | C♯ | ( ) | 4 5 6 | ( ) | 4 5 | ( ) | 5 6 |

### 6C: 2nd Inversion (Melody note is C♯)

| "Parent" Chord | | Drop 2 | | Drop 3 | | Drop 2 and 4 | |
|---|---|---|---|---|---|---|---|
| Formula | A7 | Notes | String Set | Notes | String Set | Notes | String Set |
| (3) | C♯ | C♯ | 1 2 3 | C♯ | 1 | C♯ | 1 |
| (R) | A | ( ) | 2 3 4 | ( ) | 2 | ( ) | 2 |
| (♭7) | G | ( ) | 3 4 5 | ( ) | 3 | ( ) | 4 |
| (5) | E | ( ) | 4 5 6 | ( ) | 4 | ( ) | 5 |

### 6D: 3rd Inversion (Melody note is E)

| "Parent" Chord | | Drop 2 | | Drop 3 | | Drop 2 and 4 | |
|---|---|---|---|---|---|---|---|
| Formula | A7 | Notes | String Set | Notes | String Set | Notes | String Set |
| (5) | E | E | 2 3 | E | 1 2 | E | 2 |
| (3) | C♯ | ( ) | 3 4 | ( ) | 2 3 | ( ) | 3 |
| (R) | A | ( ) | 4 5 | ( ) | 3 4 | ( ) | 5 |
| (♭7) | G | ( ) | 5 6 | ( ) | 5 6 | ( ) | 6 |

## Worksheet 2, Exercise 7 (next page)

### Layout

- Column 1: Indicates the first inversion voicings of A9, ♯9, ♭9, ♯5 and ♭5 in closed voicing with root omitted. In each case the 9th, or altered 9th, is voiced on top as the melody note. All closed voicings in Column 1 are located on the first set of four adjacent strings so that you can hear them in the context of A7 by sounding the open A string as each voicing is played.

### Procedures

- Step 1: As in Worksheet 1, write in the chord tones, where indicated, for each of the open voicings in Columns 2, 3, and 4 by applying the voicing formulas to the parent closed voicing in Column 1.

- Step 2: After completing the written portion, search for and locate the chord tones in Columns 2, 3, and 4 along their designated string sets and sound the resulting chord shapes.

**Worksheet 2**
Exercise 7 (Using A9, and various A altered dominant chords to illustrate)

| Exercise | Column 1 | | | Column 2 | | | Column 3 | | | Column 4 | | |
|---|---|---|---|---|---|---|---|---|---|---|---|---|

**7A: Dom9**

| | closed voicing (no root) | | | Drop 2 | | | Drop 3 | | | Drop 2 and 4 | | |
|---|---|---|---|---|---|---|---|---|---|---|---|---|
| | Formula | A9 | Strs. | Notes | String Set | | Notes | String Set | | Notes | String Set | |
| Melody → | (9) | B | 1 | B | 1 | 2 | B | 1 | 2 | B | 1 | 2 |
| | (♭7) | G | 2 | ( ) | 2 | 3 | ( ) | 2 | 3 | ( ) | 2 | 3 |
| | (5) | E | 3 | ( ) | 3 | 4 | ( ) | 3 | 4 | ( ) | 4 | 5 |
| | (3) | C♯ | 4 | ( ) | 4 | 5 | ( ) | 5 | 6 | ( ) | 5 | 6 |

**7B: Dom7(♯9)**

| | closed voicing (no root) | | | Drop 2 | | | Drop 3 | | | Drop 2 and 4 | | |
|---|---|---|---|---|---|---|---|---|---|---|---|---|
| | Formula | A7(♯9) | Strs. | Notes | String Set | | Notes | String Set | | Notes | String Set | |
| Melody → | (♯9) | B♯ | 1 | B♯ | 1 | 2 | B♯ | 1 | 2 | B♯ | 2 | |
| | (♭7) | G | 2 | ( ) | 2 | 3 | ( ) | 2 | 3 | ( ) | 3 | |
| | (5) | E | 3 | ( ) | 3 | 4 | ( ) | 3 | 4 | ( ) | 5 | |
| | (3) | C♯ | 4 | ( ) | 4 | 5 | ( ) | 5 | 6 | ( ) | 6 | |

**7C: Dom7(♯9♯5)**

| | closed voicing (no root) | | | Drop 2 | | | Drop 3 | | | Drop 2 and 4 | | |
|---|---|---|---|---|---|---|---|---|---|---|---|---|
| | Formula | A9 | Strs. | Notes | String Set | | Notes | String Set | | Notes | String Set | |
| Melody → | (♯9) | B♯ | 1 | B♯ | 1 | 2 | B♯ | 1 | 2 | B♯ | 1 | 2 |
| | (♭7) | G | 2 | ( ) | 2 | 3 | ( ) | 2 | 3 | ( ) | 2 | 3 |
| | (♯5) | E♯ | 3 | ( ) | 3 | 4 | ( ) | 3 | 4 | ( ) | 4 | 5 |
| | (3) | C♯ | 4 | ( ) | 4 | 5 | ( ) | 5 | 5 | ( ) | 5 | 6 |

**7D: Dom7(♯9♭5)**

| | closed voicing (no root) | | | Drop 2 | | | Drop 3 | | | Drop 2 and 4 | | |
|---|---|---|---|---|---|---|---|---|---|---|---|---|
| | Formula | A9 | Strs. | Notes | String Set | | Notes | String Set | | Notes | String Set | |
| Melody → | (♯9) | B♯ | 1 | B♯ | 1 | 2 | B♯ | 1 | 2 | B♯ | 1 | 2 |
| | (♭7) | G | 2 | ( ) | 2 | 3 | ( ) | 2 | 3 | ( ) | 2 | 3 |
| | (♭5) | E♭ | 3 | ( ) | 3 | 4 | ( ) | 3 | 4 | ( ) | 4 | 5 |
| | (3) | C♯ | 4 | ( ) | 4 | 5 | ( ) | 5 | 6 | ( ) | 5 | 6 |

**7E: Dom7(♭9)**

| | closed voicing (no root) | | | Drop 2 | | | Drop 3 | | | Drop 2 and 4 | | |
|---|---|---|---|---|---|---|---|---|---|---|---|---|
| | Formula | A7(♭9) | Strs. | Notes | String Set | | Notes | String Set | | Notes | String Set | |
| Melody → | (♭9) | B♭ | 1 | B♭ | 1 | 2 | B♭ | 1 | 2 | B♭ | 1 | 2 |
| | (♭7) | G | 2 | ( ) | 2 | 3 | ( ) | 2 | 3 | ( ) | 2 | 3 |
| | (5) | E | 3 | ( ) | 3 | 4 | ( ) | 3 | 4 | ( ) | 4 | 5 |
| | (3) | C♯ | 4 | ( ) | 4 | 5 | ( ) | 5 | 6 | ( ) | 5 | 6 |

**7F: Dom7(♭9♭5)**

| | closed voicing (no root) | | | Drop 2 | | | Drop 3 | | | Drop 2 and 4 | | |
|---|---|---|---|---|---|---|---|---|---|---|---|---|
| | Formula | A7(♭9♭5) | Strs. | Notes | String Set | | Notes | String Set | | Notes | String Set | |
| Melody → | (♭9) | B♭ | 1 | B♭ | 1 | 2 | B♭ | 1 | 2 | B♭ | 1 | 2 |
| | (♭7) | G | 2 | ( ) | 2 | 3 | ( ) | 2 | 3 | ( ) | 2 | 3 |
| | (♭5) | E♭ | 3 | ( ) | 3 | 4 | ( ) | 3 | 4 | ( ) | 4 | 5 |
| | (3) | C♯ | 4 | ( ) | 4 | 5 | ( ) | 5 | 6 | ( ) | 5 | 6 |

**7G: Dom7(♭9♯5)**

| | closed voicing (no root) | | | Drop 2 | | | Drop 3 | | | Drop 2 and 4 | | |
|---|---|---|---|---|---|---|---|---|---|---|---|---|
| | Formula | A7(♭9♯5) | Strs. | Notes | String Set | | Notes | String Set | | Notes | String Set | |
| Melody → | (♭9) | B♭ | 1 | B♭ | 1 | 2 | B♭ | 1 | 2 | B♭ | 1 | 2 |
| | (♭7) | G | 2 | ( ) | 2 | 3 | ( ) | 2 | 3 | ( ) | 2 | 3 |
| | (♯5) | E♯ | 3 | ( ) | 3 | 4 | ( ) | 3 | 4 | ( ) | 4 | 5 |
| | (3) | C♯ | 4 | ( ) | 4 | 5 | ( ) | 5 | 6 | ( ) | 5 | 6 |

# Worksheet 3, Exercise 8

## Layout

- Column 1: Indicates the third inversion voicings of "embellished" A7 chords. Embellishments include extensions 9, 10, 11, and 13 and #11 alteration. The 13th (F#) is voiced as the top melody note in all of the voicings. As in Worksheet 2, all chord voicings in Column 1 are to be played on the first set of four adjacent strings so that they can be heard in the context of A7 by sounding the open A string as each voicing is played.

## Procedures

- Same as in Worksheets 1 and 2.

**Worksheet 3**
Exercise 8 (Using a variety of extended and altered A7 chords to illustrate)

| Exercise | Column 1 | | | Column 2 | | Column 3 | | Column 4 | |
|---|---|---|---|---|---|---|---|---|---|
| **8A: Dom13** | 4-Note Closed Voicing (no root) | | | Drop 2 | | Drop 3 | | Drop 2 and 4 | |
| | Formula | A13 | Strs. | Notes | String Set | Notes | String Set | Notes | String Set |
| Melody → | 13 | (F#) | 1 | F# | 2  2  1 | F# | 1  2 | F# | 2 |
| | 10 | (C#) | 2 | ( ) | 3  4  2 | ( ) | 2  3 | ( ) | 3 |
| | 9 | (B) | 3 | ( ) | 4  5  3 | ( ) | 3  4 | ( ) | 5 |
| | b7 | (G) | 4 | ( ) | 5  6  5 | ( ) | 5  6 | ( ) | 6 |
| **8B: Dom11/13** | Closed Voicing (no root) | | | Drop 2 | | Drop 3 | | Drop 2 and 4 | |
| | Formula | A11/13 | Strs. | Notes | String Set | Notes | String Set | Notes | String Set |
| Melody → | 13 | (F#) | 1 | F# | 1  2  3 | F# | 1  2 | F# | 2 |
| | 11 | (D) | 2 | ( ) | 2  3  4 | ( ) | 2  3 | ( ) | 3 |
| | 9 | (B) | 3 | ( ) | 3  4  5 | ( ) | 3  4 | ( ) | 5 |
| | b7 | (G) | 4 | ( ) | 4  5  6 | ( ) | 5  6 | ( ) | 6 |
| **8C: Dom13(#11)** | Closed Voicing (no root) | | | Drop 2 | | Drop 3 | | Drop 2 and 4 | |
| | Formula | A13(#11) | Strs. | Notes | String Set | Notes | String Set | Notes | String Set |
| Melody → | 13 | (F#) | 1 | F# | 1  2  2 | F# | 1  2 | F# | 2 |
| | #11 | (D#) | 2 | ( ) | 2  3  3 | ( ) | 2  3 | ( ) | 3 |
| | 9 | (B) | 3 | ( ) | 3  4  5 | ( ) | 3  4 | ( ) | 5 |
| | b7 | (G) | 4 | ( ) | 4  5  6 | ( ) | 5  6 | ( ) | 6 |
| **8D: Dom13(#11) alternate voicing** | Closed Voicing (no root) | | | Drop 2 | | Drop 3 | | Drop 2 and 4 | |
| | Formula | A13(#11) | Strs. | Notes | String Set | Notes | String Set | Notes | String Set |
| Melody → | 13 | (F#) | 1 | F# | 1  2  2 | F# | 1  2  2  3 | F# | 2 |
| | #11 | (D#) | 2 | ( ) | 2  3  4 | ( ) | 2  3  3  4 | ( ) | 3 |
| | 10 | (C#) | 3 | ( ) | 3  4  5 | ( ) | 3  4  4  5 | ( ) | 5 |
| | b7 | (G) | 4 | ( ) | 4  5  6 | ( ) | 5  6  5  6 | ( ) | 6 |

# Creative Touches for Chord Voicing

## Experimenting with Inner Moving Lines and Added Tensions

The following examples use the melody and chord progression from "Alone Together," measures 11–14.

**Example 37:** "Alone Together" (excerpt, measures 11–14, basic melody and chords).

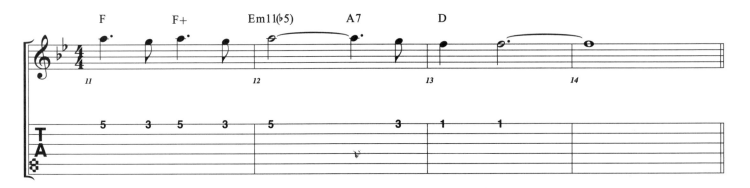

**Example 38:** "Alone Together" (excerpt, measures 11–14, harmonized melody).

Tension E is added in measure 11 to the original chord progression F to Faug—resulting in Fmaj7 to Fmaj7(♯5). Maintaining common tones F, E, and A reveals the start of a potential inner moving line as C moves chromatically to C♯.

Notice how the added tensions for Em (D), A7 (D♯), and Dmaj7 (E) in measures 12 and 13 are the result of the chromatically ascending continuation of C to C♯ in measure 11.

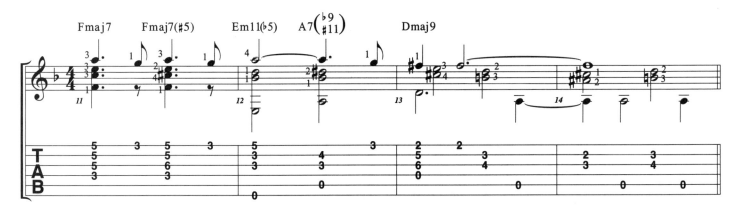

**Example 38a:** "Alone Together" (excerpt, measures 11–14, variation 1).

Chord tone E in Fmaj7 in measure 11 is treated as a possible point of origin for a descending moving line (E to E♭), which works well against the ascending line C to C♯ implied by F to Faug. Notice also how the move from E to E♭ changes the chord quality from Fmaj7(♯5) to F7(♯5).

The choice of possible tensions for Em and A7 in measure 12 is influenced by the resolution of the descending chromatic line (E, E♭, D, and C♯).

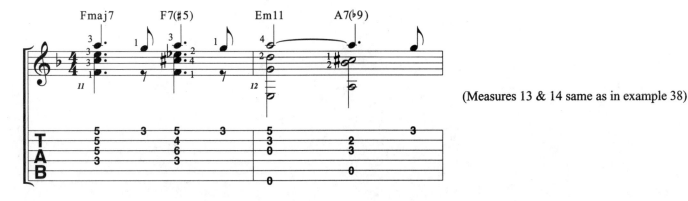

(Measures 13 & 14 same as in example 38)

**Examples 38b and 38c:** "Alone Together" (excerpt, measures 11–14, variations 2 and 3).

Varying the direction of one or more resolving tensions within a chord voicing can affect both color and mood. Notice the subtle difference in color and mood that occurs between Examples 38b and 38c as the voicings in measure 12 resolve to measure 13.

**Example 38b**

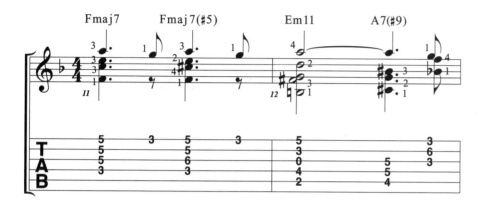

(Measures 13 & 14 same as in example 38)

**Example 38c**

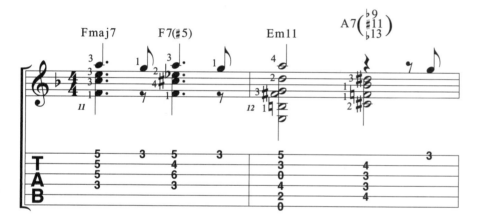

(Measures 13 & 14 same as in example 38)

# "Alone Together," version no. 1

This treatment of "Alone Together" includes examples of open- and closed-voicing formulas introduced in this chapter. You'll also find voicings that do not lend themselves to any formula. They evolve out of compromises between the requirements of the harmony and the notes availabile at a specific fingerboard location. These chord structures, often chords of omission, include fragments of extended and altered closed and open voicings, symmetrical chord shapes*, and voicings that combine open strings with fretted notes. Below, I've highlighted those measures that are also representative of a number of topics introduced in Part 2.

## 1) Chord Voicing Formulas
- Measure 1: Drop 3, Bm7(♭5)
- Measure 5: Closed voicing, Dm(maj7)
- Measure 11: Drop 2, Fmaj7, F7(♯5)
- Measure 33: Drop 2 and 4, Gm7(♭5)

## 2) Voice Leading: (Horizontal Thinking)

Measures 3–5: Each voice within the chord shape treated as a separate melody. To hear the individual voice leading:

- Play only the bass notes (D–F–E–A)
- Play only the notation directly below the melody (C–B–D–C♯)
- Play only the notation directly above the bass line (F–A–B♭)

## 3) Continuity of Phrasing

The note C♯ in Dm(maj7) sounded on the first beat of measure 5 is retained as a common tone from the A7 chord sounded on the last beat of measure 4 and introduces the melodic phrase (D–E–F–A) completed on the first beat of measure 6. Notice how the ascending middle voice (C–D–E♭–F) connecting Am7(♭5) with D7(♭9) is picked up and completed in measures 7 and 8.

## 4) Adding and Resolving Tensions to Promote Continuity

Adding tension F♯ to C7(♭9) in measure 10 creates a dissonance (♯11) that is resolved melodically with a descending moving line extended through measures 11 and 12 (F♯–F–E–E♭–D).

Adding tension F♯ to the bass voice of Gm9 in measure 32 creates a dissonance that is resolved melodically with a descending line down to D♭ in measure 33 (F♯–F–E–D–D♭). This linear resolution also helped to determine my choice of a Drop 2 and 4 voicing in second inversion for Gm7(♭5) in measure 33.

In measure 33, adding C, the 11th of Gm7(♭5) in the middle voice, made possible by the Drop 2 and 4 string configuration, creates a tension that resolves melodically in a descending line from C to B♭ on the first beat of measure 34.

## 5) Mixing Open Strings with Fretted Notes

Measure 10: Gm11 (no 5 or 9)
Measure 15: Dm6
Measure 42: A7(♭13, ♯9)

## 6) Symmetrical Chord Shapes

Measure 34: C7(♯11, ♭9), C13(♭9)

*A symmetrical chord shape is a voicing that, *without changing its shape,* can be sounded at equally distant intervals on the fingerboard to produce various extensions and/or alterations of the same basic chord.

# ALONE TOGETHER
## (Version 1)

Lyrics by
HOWARD DIETZ
Music by
ARTHUR SCHWARTZ
*Arranged by*
*HOWARD MORGEN*

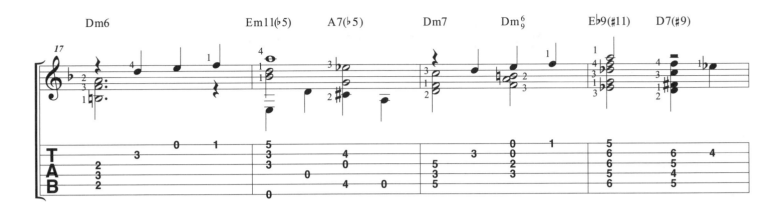

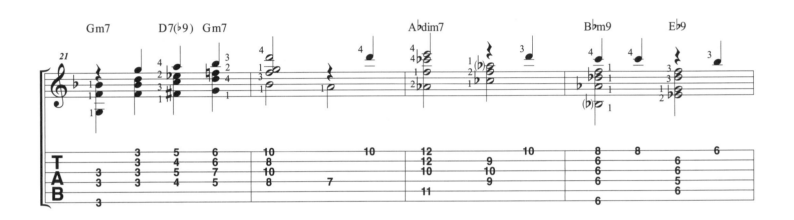

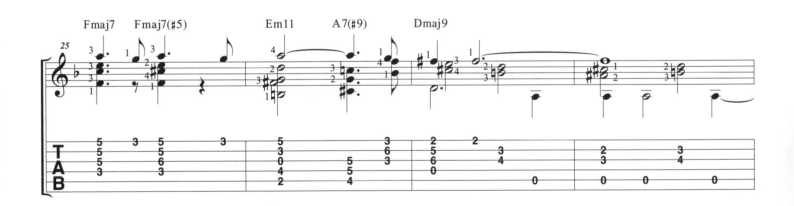

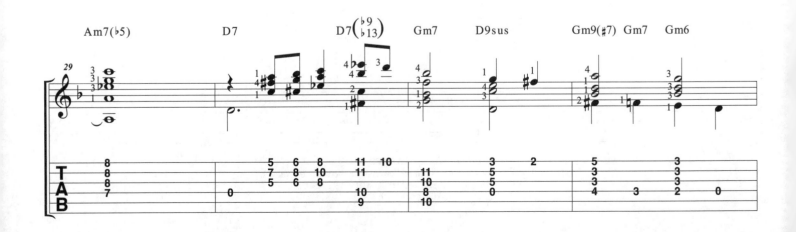

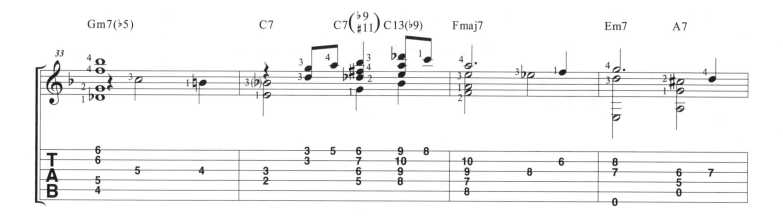

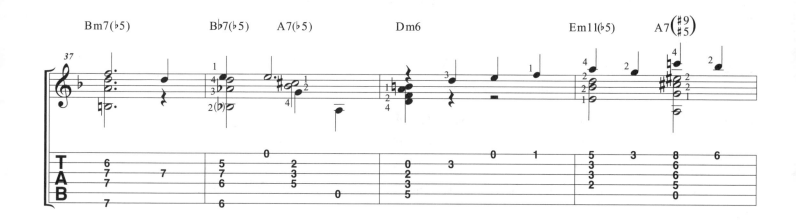

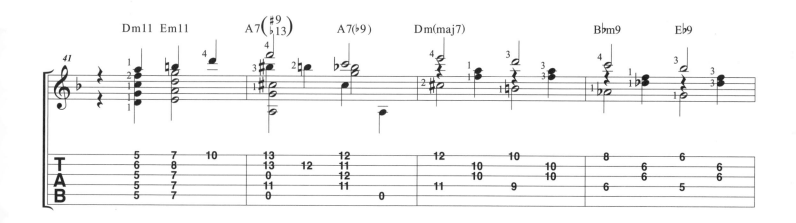

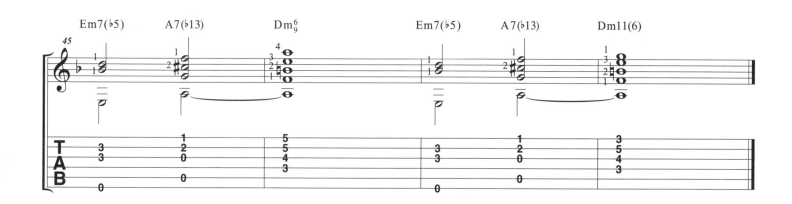

## Guide List for Chapter 7

See the Master Guide List at the end of the book for publisher and item number information for each book.

### *Drop-2 Concept for Guitar,* **Charles Chapman**
Chord Voicing, pages 6–59.

### *Solo Jazz Guitar Method,* **Barry Greene**
Chord voicing, pages 8–11.

### *Chord Chemistry,* **Ted Greene**
Advanced chord voice leading concepts and reference charts, pages 17–54.

### *Mel Bay's Complete Book of Harmony, Theory and Voice Leading,* **Bret Willmott**
Drop 2 voicings applied enharmonically as extensions and alterations, pages 8–14.
Voice leading, pages, 14–16.
Tensions, pages 21–26.

### *Modern Chord Progressions,* **Ted Greene**
Advanced chord voicings and voice leading concepts.

### *Almanac of Guitar Voice Leading Vols. I & II,* **Mick Goodrick**
Advanced chord voicings and voice leading for guitarists, arrangers, and all instruments.

### *Jazz Guitar Harmony,* **Jody Fisher**
Voice leading, adding tensions with extensions, altered chords, and symmetrical chord shapes, pages 50–57.

# Chapter 8:
# All About Chord Symbols

## How to Crack the Code

There are two types of chord symbols in use today, **slash** and **standard**. Slash chord symbols are the easiest to interpret, especially for suggesting bass lines, for example: B7(♯9)/D♯. They provide the chord letter name (root), quality (major, minor, dominant), tension tones (13, 9, 11, ♯5, ♭9, etc.) and inversion, shown as a letter placed to the right of the slash indicating the bass note. When slash chords are present, chord symbols not accompanied by a slash are assumed to be in root position.

**Example 39:** Slash chords indicating the progression and suggested bass line for the first two measures of "'Round Midnight."

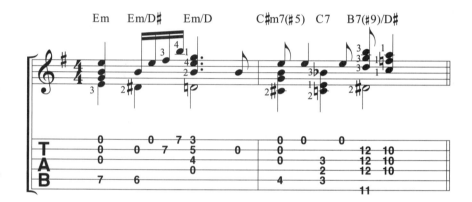

Standard chord symbols also provide the chord root, quality and tensions but unlike slash chord symbols, do not include the chord inversion. When viewed as isolated finger "grips," standard chord symbols, like snapshots, can reflect only a small segment of an entire chord progression. However, **when viewed in groups of at least three or more at a time**, standard chord symbols can be very helpful for indicating inner voice movement and moving bass lines.

> *The linear, horizontal interrelationship among chords in a progression is often overlooked because of the habit acquired early on of treating chord symbols as isolated, unrelated finger grips. In this sense, standard chord symbols function like a code for what is occurring in the harmony, for guitarists who generally aren't taught how to crack the code!*

# Seven Approaches for Finding the Differences Between Standard Chord Symbols

Just as the motion we perceive in a movie is produced by the relative difference in position of the various elements within individual movie frames, the movement of individual voices within chords in a progression is discerned by the differences between consecutive chord symbols (frames).

The following procedures are based on two principles:

The **first two symbols** in a group of three or more often signal both the presence of, and the direction for, a potential moving line.

Try to keep moving lines moving **in the same direction** for as long as possible.

## Approach I: Spell Out and Compare Adjacent Chord Symbols

> Step 1: Write in the spelling of each consecutive chord and place above its corresponding chord symbol. See Figure 30.

**Figure 30:** Chord progression implying an ascending moving line.

> Step 2: Cancel common tones (note how this procedure reveals the direction of an ascending moving line). See Figure 30a.

**Figure 30a**

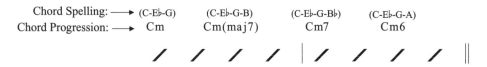

Figure 31 is similar to above, but will reveal a descending moving line.

**Figure 33**

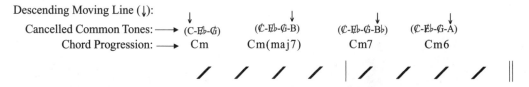

Cancellation of common tones reveals the descending moving line. See Figure 31a.

**Figure 31a**

Descending Moving Line (↓):
Cancelled Common Tones: ⟶ (C-E♭-G̷)   (C̷-E♭-G̷-B)   (C̷-E♭-G̷-B♭)   (C̷-E♭-G̷-A)
Chord Progression: ⟶   Cm       Cm(maj7)      Cm7          Cm6

Once the direction of a moving line has been established by the first two chord symbols, choose the *closest* note in each successive chord symbol that **maintains its direction.**

Figure 32 is a chord progression with an inner descending moving line.

**Figure 32**

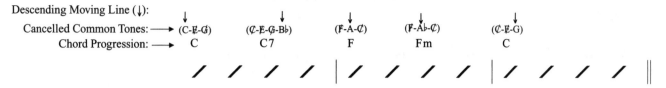

Figure 33 is a chord progression that reveals an inner ascending line.

**Figure 33**

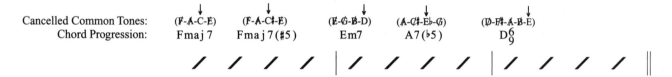

In Exercises 9 and 9a, find the descending moving line.

Start on the note C and, using arrows, indicate the descending line in Exercise 9.

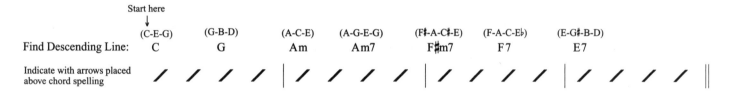

Start on the note A♭ and, using arrows, indicate the descending line in Exercise 9a.

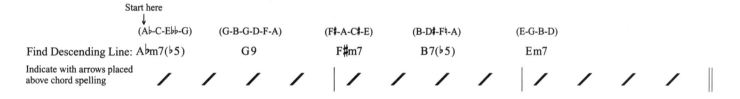

# Spotting Moving Lines in Real Time

While spelling out and comparing standard chord symbols is helpful for visualizing and graphically revealing moving lines, it's too time consuming a process for real time performance. In real time, moving lines need to be spotted and applied at a glance.

## Approach II: Look for Adjacent Chord Symbols with Common Tone Roots

For Example:

- C–Cmaj7 or Cm–Cm(maj7) = root down a half step to 7

- C–C7 or Cm–Cm7 = root down a whole step to ♭7

- C–Cm = 3rd down a half step to ♭3

- C7–Cdim7 = 3rd down a half step to ♭3, 5th down a half step to ♭5, ♭7 down a half step to ♭♭7.

- C–Caug, Cm–Cm(♯5), C7 to C7(♯5) = 5th up a half step to ♯5.

In Example 40, look for the descending stepwise linear motion of the root to the ♭7 (C to C7) voiced as a bass line. The remaining chords in the progression, F–Fm–C, are voiced to accommodate the direction of the line.

### Example 40

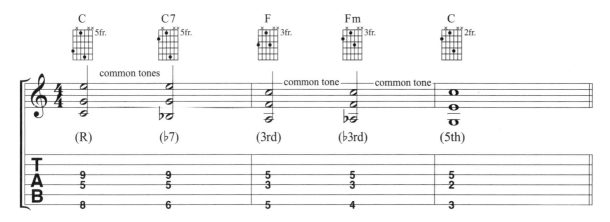

Example 40a uses the same approach as Example 40 for Cm to Cm7.

### Example 40a

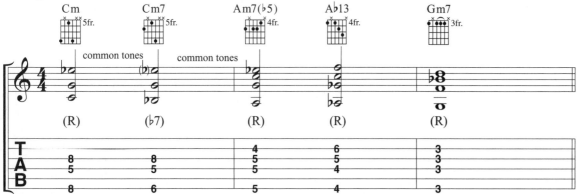

**Approach III: Look for Diatonic and Chromatic Chord Progressions**

Diatonic and chromatic root movement often yields more than one moving line. You can quickly access these lines by voicing each successive chord within the progression in root position.

Notice the multiple lines in Examples 41 and 41a as the four voices within each chord resolve to the chord that follows.

**Example 41**

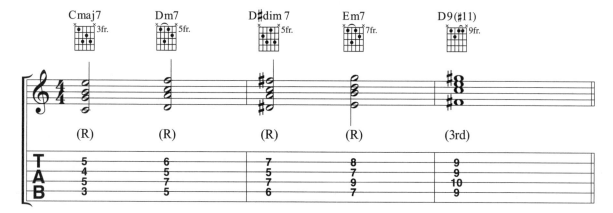

**Example 41a**

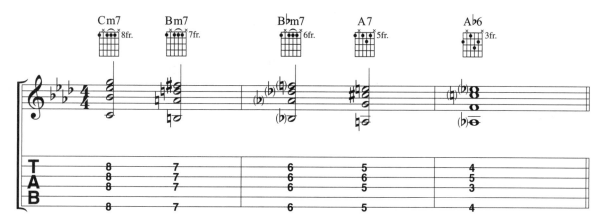

## Approach IV: Look for Cycle Patterns

The chord progressions of most popular songs contain chord sequences with two or more successive chords whose roots move counterclockwise through the Cycle of 5ths. See Figure 34.

### Root Movement

### Cycle of 5ths

### (Chord qualities can be major, minor, or dominant)

Figure 34:

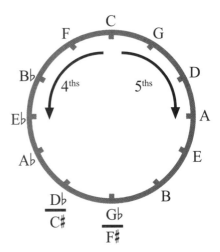

Cycle Patterns: Three or more successive chord roots following the Cycle of 5ths *counterclockwise* (in 4ths) are called a "cycle pattern." (To help memorize cycle pattern movement think "B-E-A-D": Bb-Eb-Ab-Db and B-E-A-D.)

**Example 42:** Cycle pattern of dominant 7th chords.

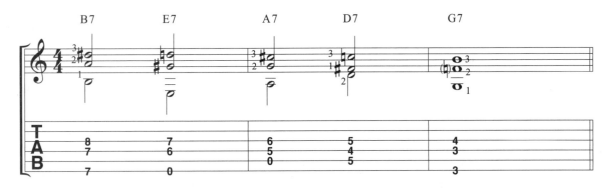

Cycle patterns with dominant 7th chords can be implied by either skipwise or stepwise moving lines. In general, skipwise lines, either down a perfect 5th or its inversion up a perfect 4th, are most effective in the bass voice as the root of successive dominant 7th chords. See Example 43.

Example 43

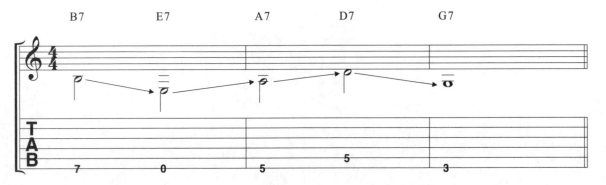

Stepwise lines in a cycle pattern descend chromatically either as 3 to ♭7 or ♭7 to 3. They can be employed as bass lines but are generally most effective among the inner voices. See Examples 44 and 44a.

**Example 44:** Stepwise motion (3 to ♭7).

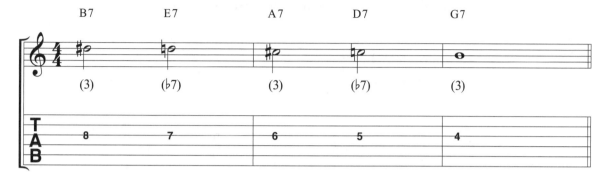

**Example 44a:** Stepwise motion (♭7 to 3).

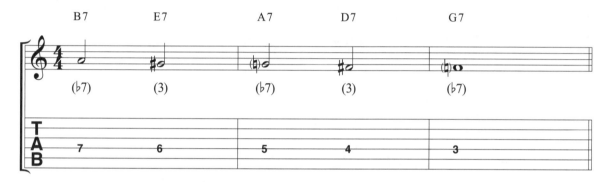

When both of the above, chromatically descending stepwise lines are sounded simultaneously, a tritone (augmented 4th/diminished 5th) interval is produced which can imply a cycle pattern of dominant 7th chords. (See Part 1, Chapter 3)

**Example 45:** Tritone shapes descending chromatically.

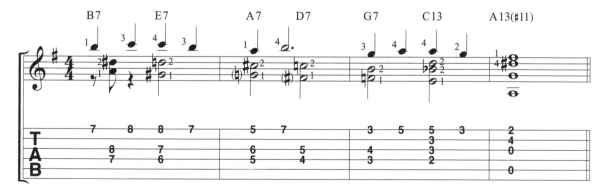

**Example 45a:** Excerpt from "Nice Work If You Can Get It" with cycle pattern B7–E7–A7–D7–G7–C (See Part 1, Chapter 3).

**Example 46:** An excerpt from "Stardust" Version 2 *(see page 158).*

Look for the cycle patterns Fm9–B♭7–E♭maj7–A♭maj7 and Dm7–G7–Cmaj7, voiced with skipwise root movement in the bass line (measures 25–27). Also note the diatonic and chromatic chord progression: Cmaj7–Dm7–D♯dim7–Em7, resolving to D9(♭5), voiced with an ascending chromatic stepwise moving line in the bass voice.

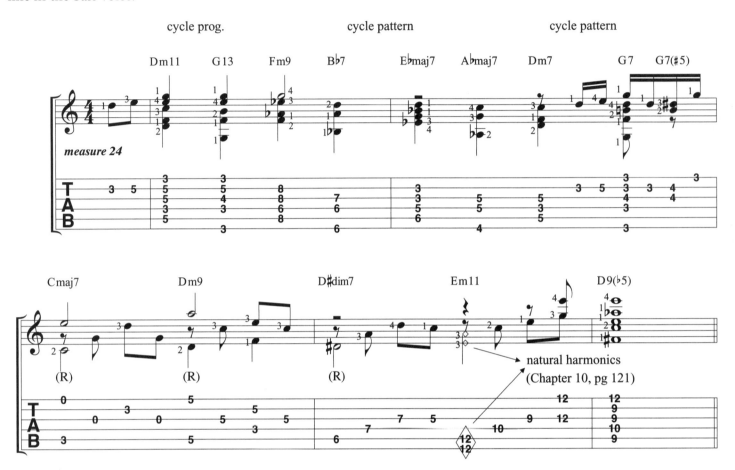

## Approach V: Look for Line-Dependent Patterns

Line-dependent patterns are built around, and follow the movement of, ascending and descending stepwise moving lines. Most line-dependent patterns are easy to spot at a glance since **at least three of four or five consecutive chord symbols share a common root letter name.**

To quickly access the moving line in the following line-dependent pattern maintain a common-tone C in the bass voice of each successive chord. The implied moving line will be revealed in an inner voice. See Example 47.

**Example 47**

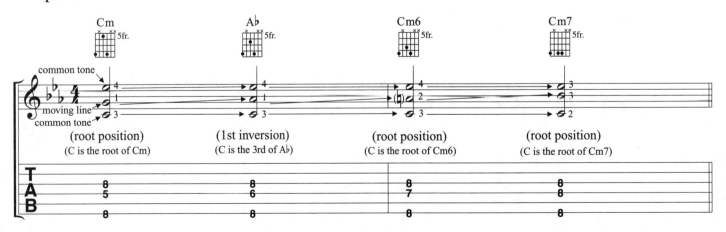

With the common tone C maintained in the bass voice, the moving line G–A♭–A–B♭ is revealed. Notice that Cm–A♭–Cm6–Cm7, actually implies one harmony (C minor) with embellishments ♯5, 6, ♭7, generated by the moving line itself. That's why many line-dependent patterns often share a common root—the A♭ chord could be thought of as Cm(♯5).

Once a moving line is revealed, it can be placed among the inner voices (Example 47a) or employed as a bass line (Example 47b).

**Example 47a**

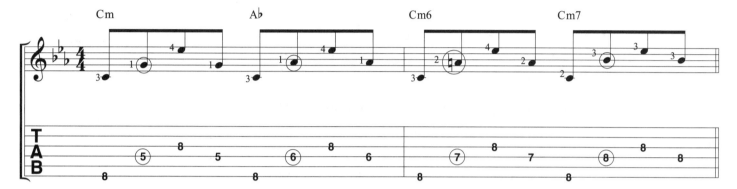

**Example 47b**

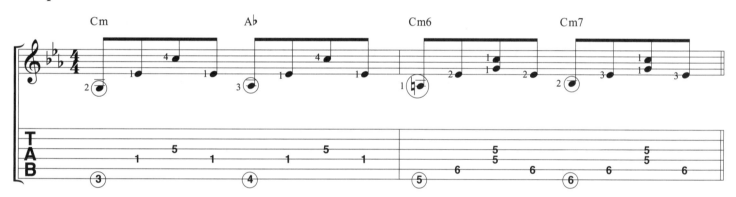

Example 48 deals with a line-dependent pattern derived from Cm–Cm(maj7)–Cm7–Cm6–A♭maj7 with voicings in root position. Common tones C, E♭, and G reveal a descending stepwise moving line among the inner voices on the 3rd string.

**Example 48**

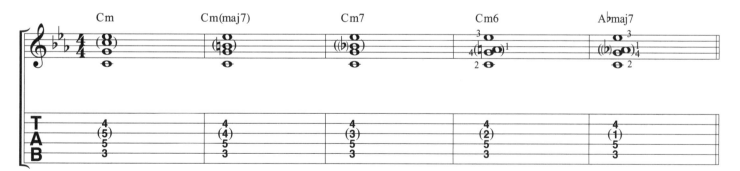

Here is the same line-dependent progression as Example 48 with common tones E♭ and G in the upper voices. The remaining non-common tones are voiced as a chromatically descending bass line.

**Example 48a**

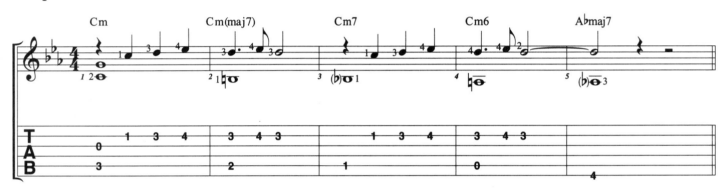

Here is the bass line from Example 48a applied to the first five measures of "My Funny Valentine."

**Example 49**

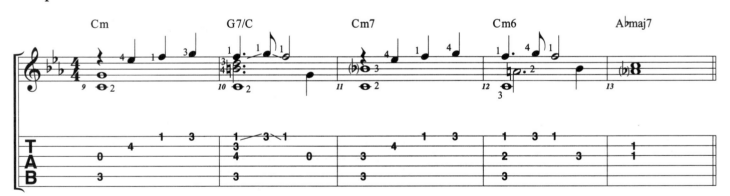

Example 49a shows how maintaining common tone C as a "pedal" tone in the bass voice for measures 9–13 of "My Funny Valentine" reveals a descending stepwise line in measures 10–13 (B–B♭–A–A♭).

**Example 49a**

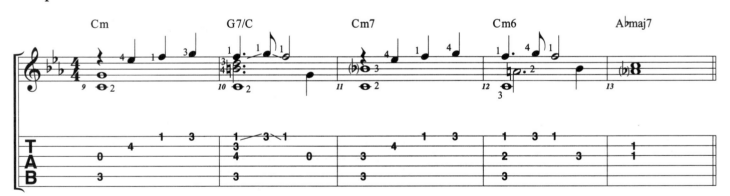

# Spotting Moving Lines in Less Obvious Chord Patterns

## Approach VI: Look for Non Line-Dependent Chord Patterns

Maintaining a common tone other than the root in the bass voice can reveal moving lines that do not share roots in common.

Example 50 is the chord progression from the first two measures of "Body and Soul" voiced with common tone B in the bass—B is the 5th of Em, the root of B7(♭13), the 5th of Em7 and the 9th of A9(♭13).

**Example 50**

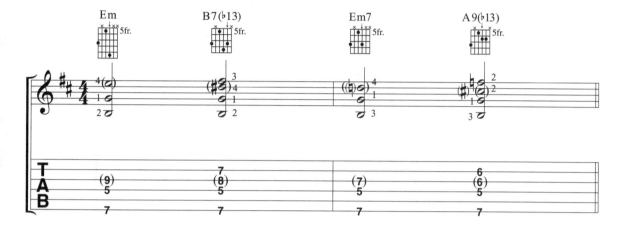

This next example shows how we can use the same inner moving line as a bass line to the first three measures of "Body and Soul."

**Example 50a**

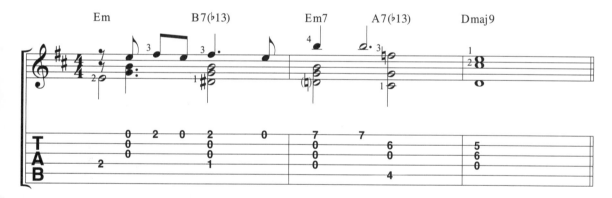

**Approach VII: Look for Adjacent Chord Shapes** (a graphic way of viewing adjacent chord symbols on the fingerboard)

Try to voice the first two chord **shapes** in a group of three or more standard chord symbols, so that at least one of the chord tones in both shapes shares the **same** string and fret placement on the fingerboard. The movement of the remaining tones as the first shape resolves to the second, will reveal the direction of the moving line(s).

**Figure 35**

C to G

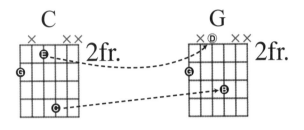

Common tone G maintained
at the 3rd fret, 6th string:

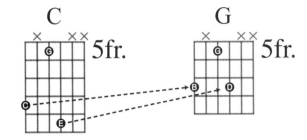

Common tone G maintained
at the 5th fret, 4th string:

You can see that this reveals two potential moving lines as C resolves to G.

Question: Which of the two moving lines extracted from Figure 35 (C–B or E–D) would work best as a bass line for the following chord progression?

**Figure 36**

| | C | G | Am | Am7 | F#m7(♭5) | F7 | E7 |
|---|---|---|---|---|---|---|---|
| | / | / | / | / | / | / | / / |
| **Bass line:** | ( ) | ( ) | (A) | (G) | (F#) | (F) | (E) |

Example 51 is the chord progression of Figure 36 as an accompaniment with the moving line voiced in the bass.

**Example 51**

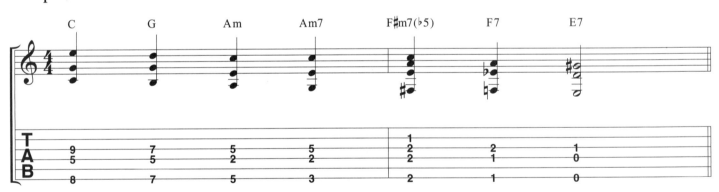

Example 51a shows the chord progression and bass line from Example 51 voiced below the melody from measures 43 and 44 of "Stardust," version no. 2 (see page 161). Notice that the bass line is voiced one octave higher than in the previous example.

**Example 51a**

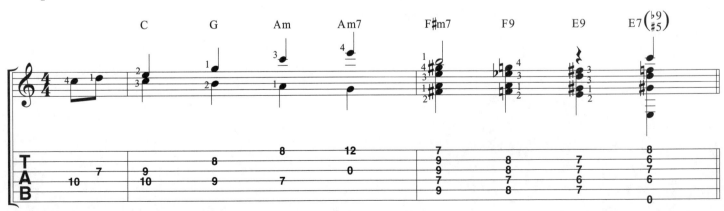

The chord progressions of the following treatments of "My Funny Valentine," version no. 1 and "Body and Soul," version no. 1 contain examples of adjacent chords with common tone roots, line dependent and non line-dependent chord patterns, cycle patterns and chord sequences with diatonic and chromatic root movement—all generating moving lines using the approaches suggested in this chapter.

Once potential moving lines have been revealed, it is up to you to find ways for weaving them into the fabric of your arrangement. Here are three approaches for the first three measures of "Body and Soul," version no. 1.

**Example 52:** Chord-melody style.

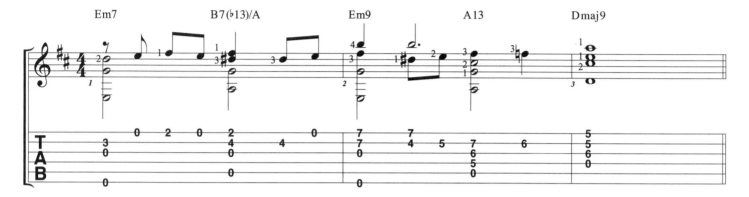

**Example 52a:** Melody sandwiched among inner voices with accompaniment both above and below.

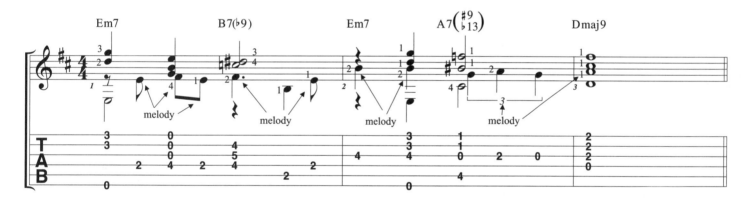

**Example 52b:** Another chord-melody approach. (Note the chord addition of B♭7(♭5) in measure 1, see Chapter 9, Chord Substitution).

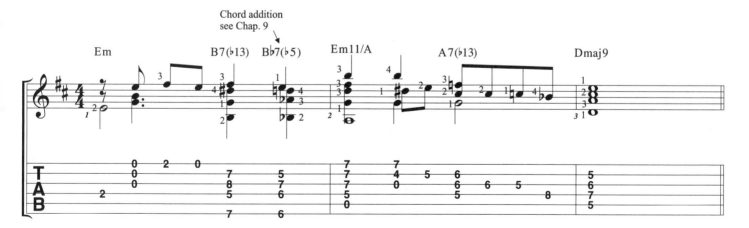

# MY FUNNY VALENTINE
## (Version 1)

Words by
LORENZ HART
Music by
RICHARD RODGERS
*Arranged by*
*HOWARD MORGEN*

**Slowly, freely**

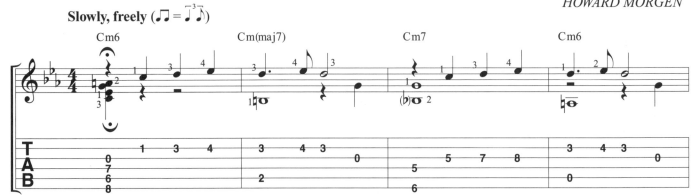

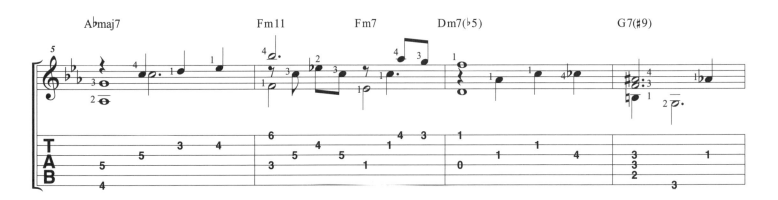

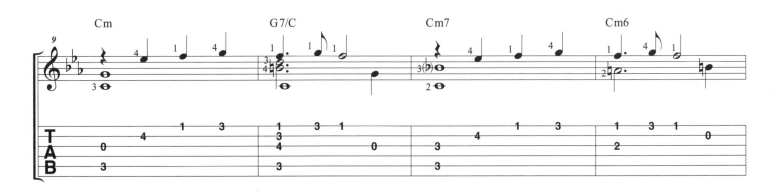

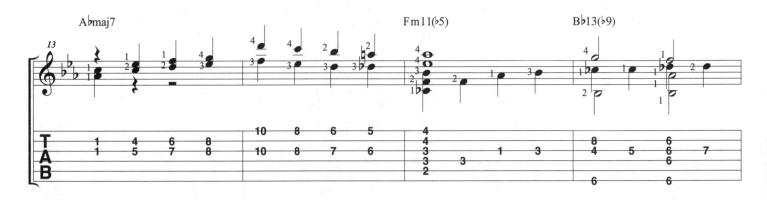

# BODY AND SOUL
## (Version 1)

Words by
EDWARD HEYMAN, ROBERT SOUR
and FRANK EYTON
Music by
JOHN GREEN
*Arranged by*
*HOWARD MORGEN*

**Slowly, freely**

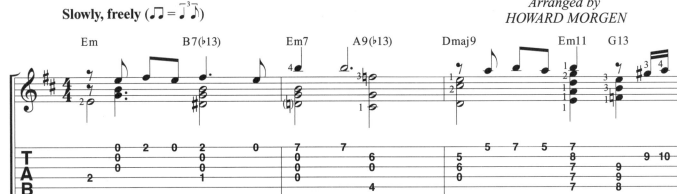

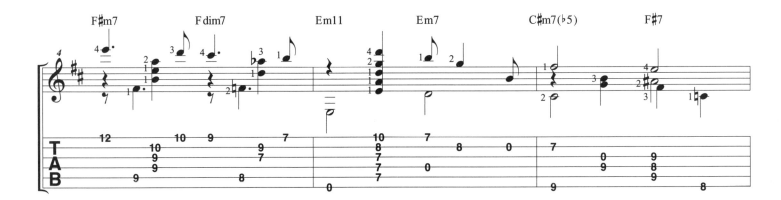

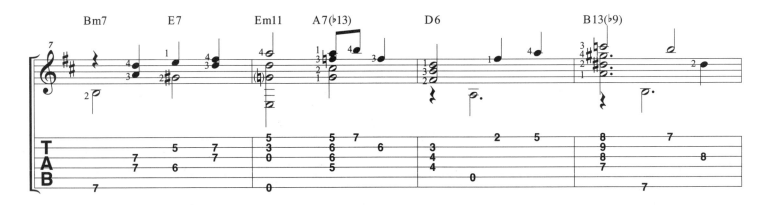

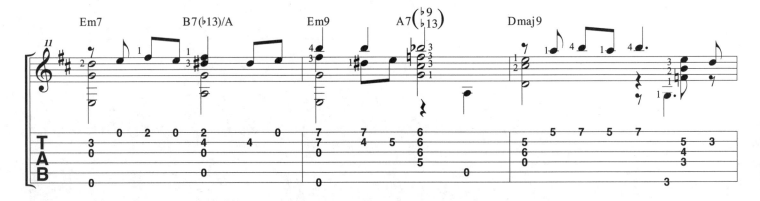

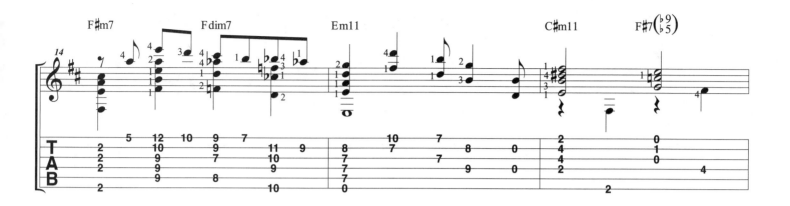

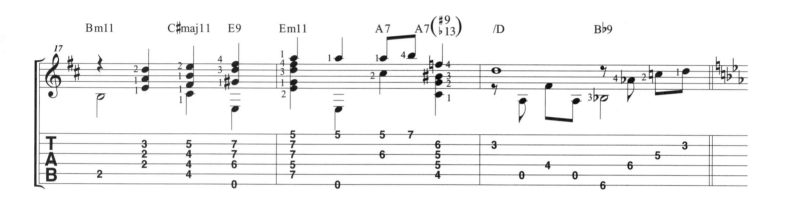

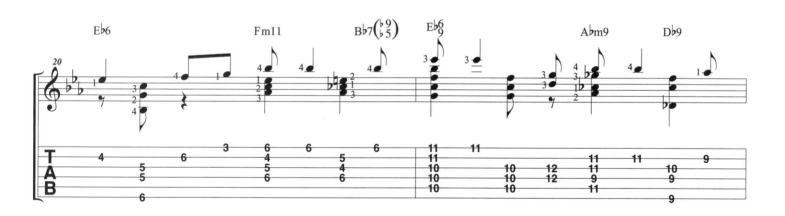

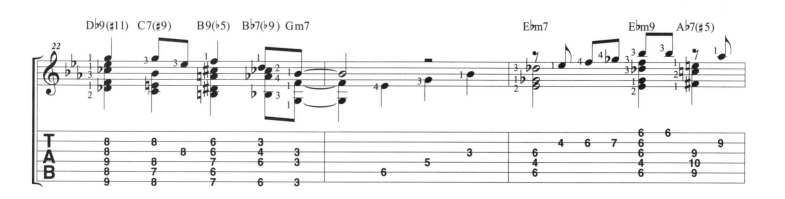

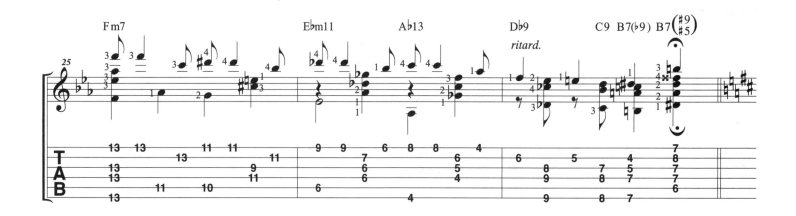

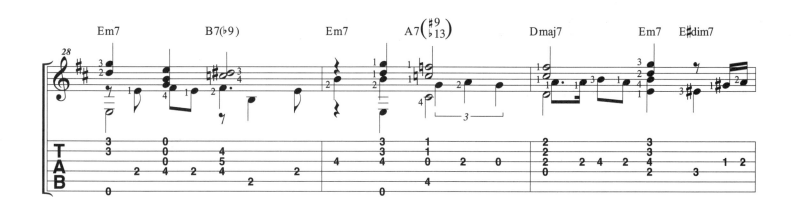

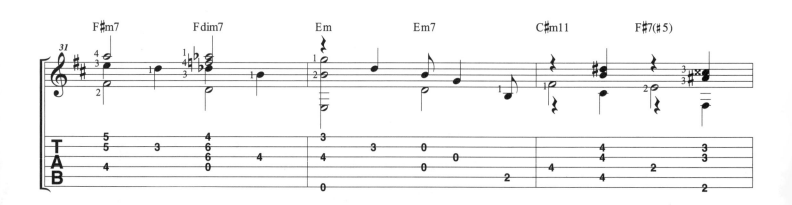

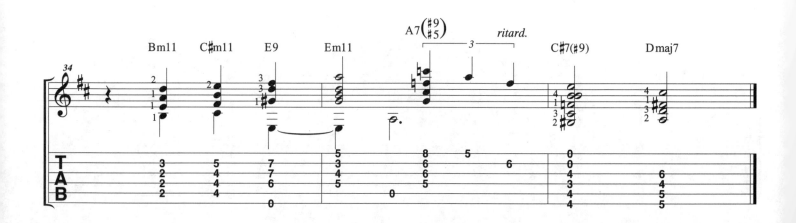

# Guide List for Chapter 8

See the Master Guide List at the end of the book for publisher and item number information for each book.

*Concepts: Arranging for Fingerstyle Guitar,* **Howard Morgen**
How to find inner moving lines and walking bass lines with the aid of chord symbols, pages 36–63.

*Howard Morgen's Solo Guitar (Insights, Arranging Techniques & Classic Jazz Standards)*
*All About Chord Progressions,* **Jim Ferguson and Howard Morgen**
Root movement, cycle patterns, line-dependent patterns, secondary dominants, cycle-based chromatic patterns, and much more, pages 86–116.

*Chord Chemistry,* **Ted Greene**
Systematic thinking, pages 68–74.

*Alfred's Just Jazz Real Book*
*Alfred's Just Standards Real Book*
Both books feature classic standards from the great American songbook, (including all the song titles featured in this book) with original lyrics, progressions, and suggested chord substitutions clearly and accurately presented.

*Fingerboard Breakthrough,* **(video), Howard Morgen**

# Chapter 9:
# Chord Substitution and Chord Addition

Using chord substitution and chord addition can add subtle touches of interest and even surprise to often-heard songs. Chord substitution refers to the replacement of any chord by a chord with a different root and/or a different quality. See Example 53.

**Example 53:** Original progression.

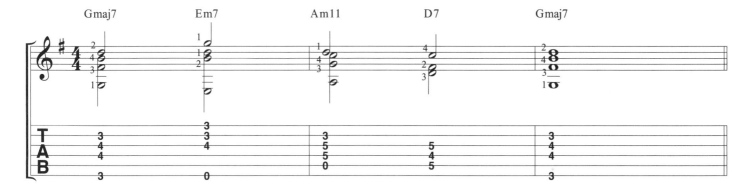

**Example 53:** Substitute progression.

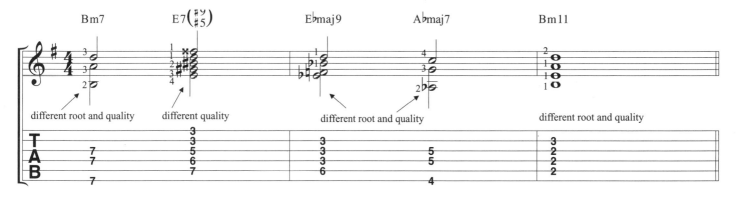

**Note:** Chords with a different root may be of either the same or a different quality as the chords they replace.

## Tritone Substitution (TT): The "♭5" Principle

Provided there is no conflict with the melody*, any chord can be replaced by another chord whose root is the flatted 5th of the chord it replaces. See Figure 37.

**Figure 37**

Original Progression:    /Dm7  /G7      /Cmaj7//
With Substitution:       /Dm7  /D♭7    /Cmaj7//

Notice that the root of the D♭7 chord is a flatted 5th from the root of the G7 chord that it is substituting.

This substitution process above is called **tritone substitution** because the root of the original chord and its substitute are exactly three whole tones apart (three whole steps is a diminished 5th, also known as an augmented 4th). Since both roots are equally distant, the roots of each chord can be reversed and become chord substitutions for each other. (D♭7 can substitute for G7 and G7 can substitute for D♭7.) See Figure 38.

*In the absence of a melody part, such as in a turnaround, there are many possible substitutions for any given chord. However, once a melody part is present the number of possible substitutions is drastically reduced. For this reason, you always need to test your substitution choices by ear against the melody part.*

**Figure 38**

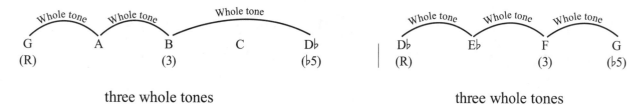

Common tones are the basis for all chord substitutions. In Figure 39 below, you can see that G7 and D♭7 both share the notes B and F. Dominant 7th chords with root notes a tritone apart always share the same 3rd and 7th. See Figure 39.

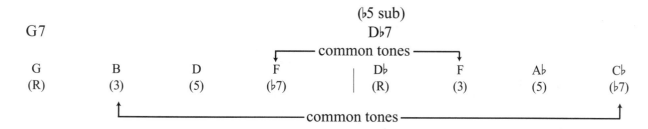

Note that the 3rd of G7 is the ♭7 of D♭7.
Note that the ♭7 of G7 is the 3rd of D♭7.

Note that the 3rd and the 7th "flip"—the 3rd and 7th of the G7 become the 7th and 3rd of D♭7.

Following are two examples of tritone substitution using the chord progression from "Alone Together" as a basis.

**Example 54:** Original progression.

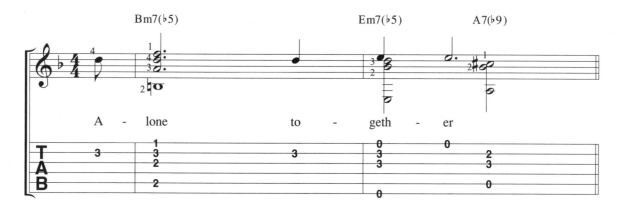

With tritone substitution:

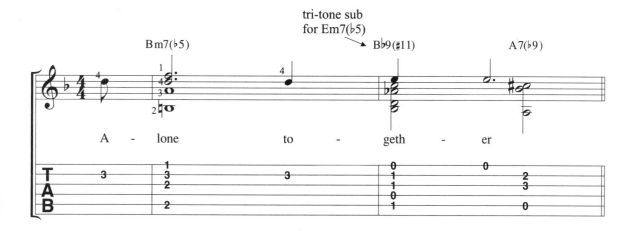

**Example 55:** Original progression.

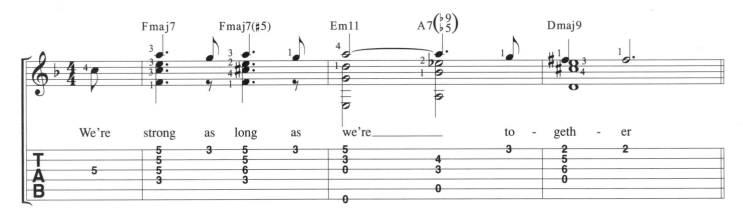

With tritone substitution.

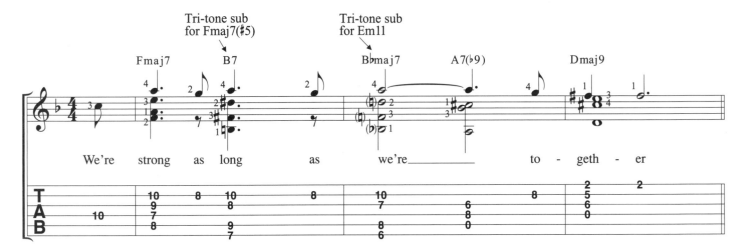

# Substitution of Minor 7th Chord for a Dominant 7th

Any dominant 7th chord can be replaced by a minor 7th built from the 5th of the dominant 7th it replaces. For example, here is the original progression from "Li'l Darlin'."

**Example 56**

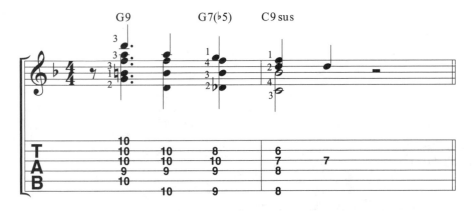

**Example 56a**

In this next example, we substitute Dm7 (on beat 3) for G9?

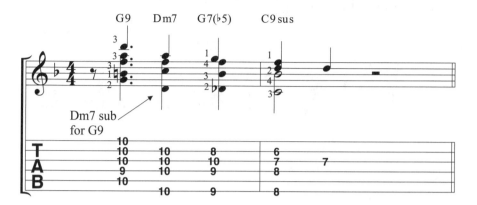

**Example 56b**

In this next variation, we use the tritone sub for G9 [Db7(#11)] on beat 4.

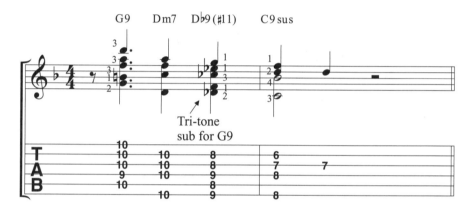

# Substitution with Relative Major and Minor Chords

For major chords, you can try substituting either the **relative minor** (vi) or the **secondary relative minor** (iii).

**Figure 40**

| Fmaj7 | Gm7 | **Am7** | Bbmaj7 | C7 | **Dm7** | Em7(b5) |
|-------|-----|---------|--------|-----|---------|---------|
| Imaj7 | ii7 | **iii7** | IVmaj7 | V7 | **vi7** | vii7 |
|       |     | **(SRM)** |       |     | **(RM)** |        |

Notice that Am7 and Dm7 each share three tones in common with Fmaj7:

Fmaj7: F–A–C–E     Am7: A–C–E–G     Dm7: D–F–A–C

To find the relative minor, think down a minor 3rd (3 frets) from the major chord root (F major down three frets to Dm). To find the secondary relative minor, think up a major 3rd (4 frets) from the chord root (F major up to Am).

There are two possible major chord substitutions for a minor 7th chord. To find the relative major think up a minor 3rd (3 frets: Dm up to F major). To find the secondary relative major think down a major 3rd (4 frets: Dm down to B major).

**Question:** What are two possible chord substitutions for Am7?

**Answer:** C major and F major. Am7 is the relative minor of C major and Am7 is the secondary relative minor of F major.

**Example 57**

Below is an excerpt from "Speak Low," first with the original progression and then with substitutions: Am7 replaces the original Fmaj7, and Dmaj13 replaces the original B♭m11.

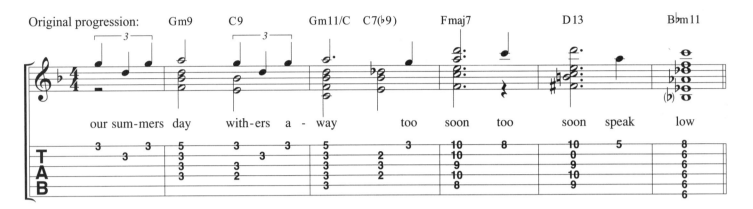

**Example 57a**

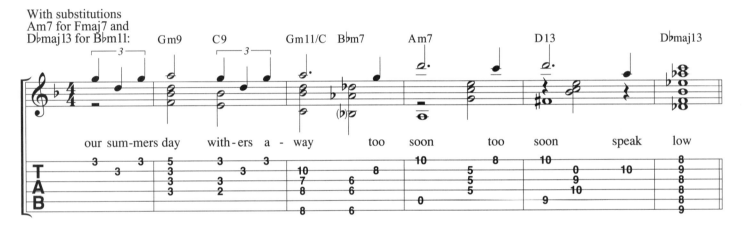

**Note:** The B♭m7 on beat 3 of measure 3 is a chromatic passing chord to Am7; the Am7 on beat 1 of measure 4 is the secondary relative minor of Fmaj7; and the D♭maj7 on the last beat is the relative major of B♭m.

## Chromatic Approach Chords

**Any chord can be approached by a substitute chord of any quality whose root is located a half step either above or below.** The quality of the "approach" chord can be determined by ear and depends, as always, upon the melody and harmonic context.

Below are excerpts from "Body and Soul" showing the original progression and suggested substitutions. A chromatic approach chord (G13), located a half step above F♯m7 replaces the original Em7.

**Example 58:** Original progression.

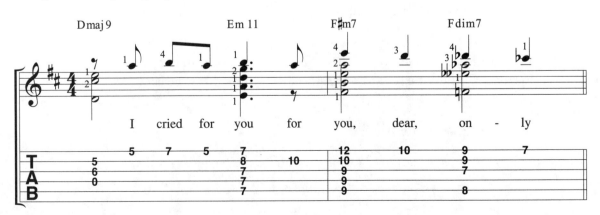

**Example 58a:** With substitutions.

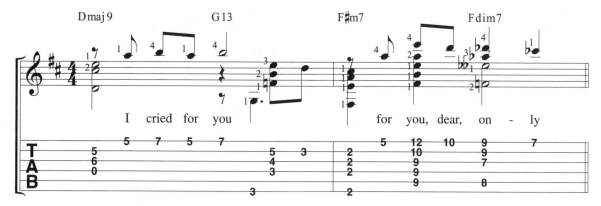

Below are two excerpts from "The More I See You" showing the original progression and substitutions.

**Example 59:** Original progression.

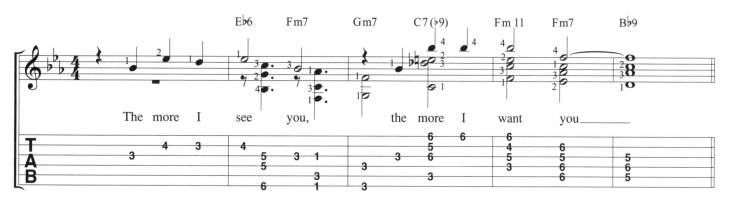

In Example 59A the tritone of E♭[Am7(♭5)] replaces the original E♭6. Am7(♭5) can also be thought of as a chromatic approach chord to A♭9. Chromatic approach chord A♭9 replaces the original Fm7 and chromatic approach chord Bm9(♯11) replaces the original Fm7. B9(♯11) is also a tritone sub for Fm.

**Example 59a:** With substitutions.

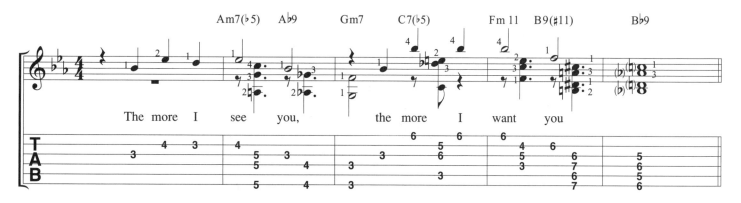

# Melodic Common Tone Substitution

Based on the common tone principle of chord substitution, any note can be temporarily considered the root, 7, ♭7, 6, ♯5, 5, ♯4, 4, etc. of any chord quality. This fact makes it possible to systematically search *by ear* for potential substitutions above and below any given melody note from among a wide variety of chord roots and qualities. For example, melody note A could be the root of A6, the 7th of B♭maj7, the flat 7th of B7, the 6th of C6, etc.

Next we will look at an excerpt from "Alone Together," again showing the original progression and possible substitutions.

Notice that in the substitution version the melody note E on the first beat is treated as the 11th of Bm11 (replacing the original A♭dim7) and is followed by E7(♭9)—enharmonic to A♭dim7. In the next measure, the original Gm11 chord followed by a passing chord is then followed by a B♭m9 chord replacing the original C7(♭9). A B♭m9 supporting melody note C on the first beat of the measure could also have been substituted for the original Gm11. Try it!

**Example 60:** Original progression.

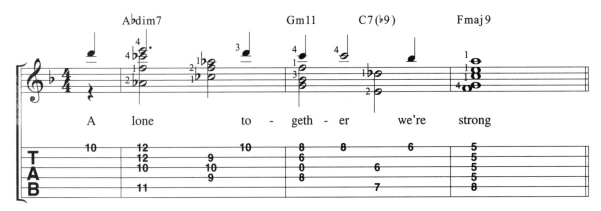

**Example 60a:** With substitutions.

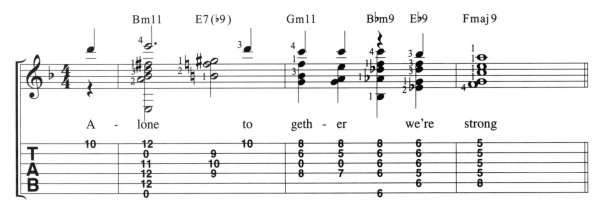

Examples 61 and 61a indicate the original progression for the final measures of "My Foolish Heart." Example 61a shows a Bmaj13 replacing the original B♭6/9 for the first two beats of the final measure (Bmaj13 could also be thought of as a chromatic approach chord to B♭6/9).

**Example 61**                    **Example 61A**

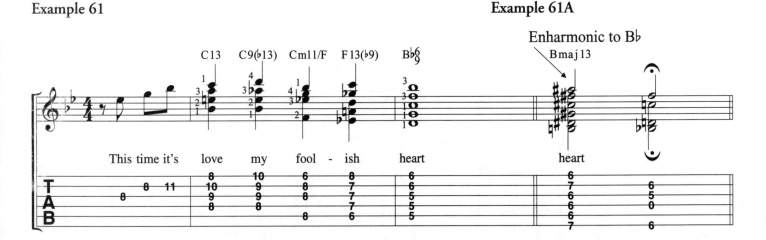

# Chord Addition

Chord additions differ from chord substitutions in that they do not replace chords, instead we are adding more chords to the progression.

**Example 62:** Original chord progression from "Stardust."

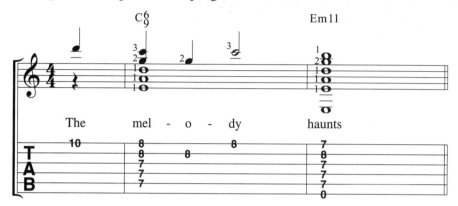

**Example 62a:** Chord addition of F9 (a chromatic approach chord to Em11) adds a "bluesy" effect. Note: this excerpt is from "Stardust," version no. 2.

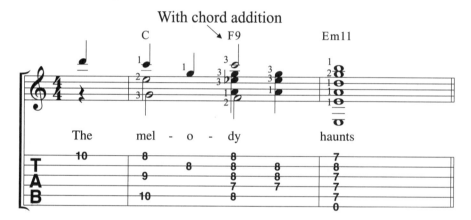

**Example 63:** Original progression from "Stardust."

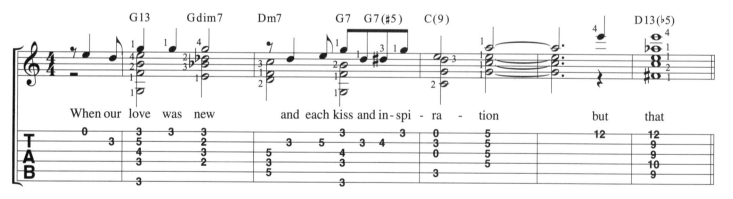

**Example 63a:** With chord additions and substitutions.

Lots of harmonic interest occurs when cycle pattern F–Bb–Eb–Ab is added to the original progression. (The common tone melody note G is treated as the 9th of Fm9 at the start of the cycle pattern.) Notice also how scalewise diatonic and chromatic chord additions C(9), Dm9, D♯dim7, and Em7 help to increase the rate and flow of chord changes during a static portion of the original progression. Chord substitutions include Dm7 for the original G7 and a Db9 tritone sub for G9.

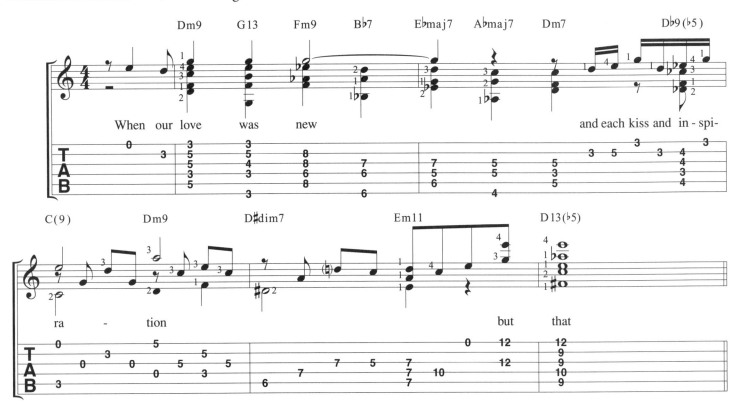

# Backcycling

**Backcycling** is a re-harmonization technique that is useful for finding chord additions and chord substitutions. It's based on the tendency of chord roots to resolve either down a perfect 5th or, its inversion, up a perfect 4th. For example, G can resolve down a perfect 5th to C or up a perfect 4th—again to C.

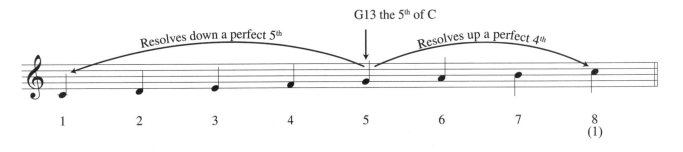

In order to more clearly visualize the backcycling process, I've used diagrams of the Cycle of 4ths in clockwise motion rather than the Cycle of 5ths in counter-clockwise motion. The progression and resolution of root movement remains the same.

**Figures 41 and 41a:** Figure 41 shows the Cyle of 4ths. Figure 41a shows how we can "backcycle" to add chords.

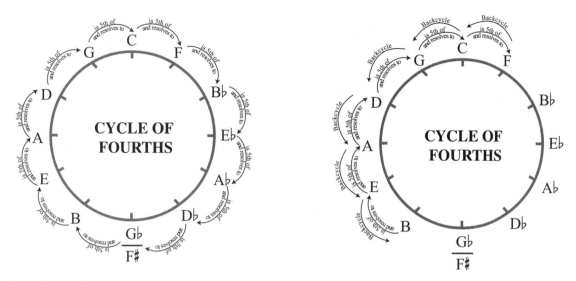

## Backcycling for Chord Addition:

Step 1: Select from any ***odd** numbered measure a temporary goal chord (T.G.) to which the first chord addition will resolve.

**Figure 42:** Static chord progression.

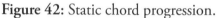

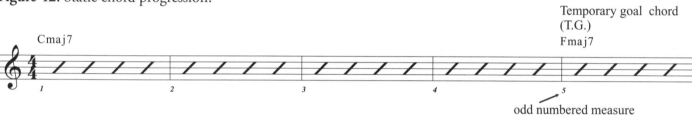

Step 2: Working backwards from right to left (see Figure 41a), place C (the 5th of F) to the left of Fmaj7 to become the root tone of the first chord addition.

**Figure 42a:** Backcycling from Fmaj7.

Step 3: Continue backcycling from **right to left** with the root tone of each new chord addition becoming in turn a temporary goal chord from which to backcycle.

**Figure 42b:** Backcycling from each new chord addition.

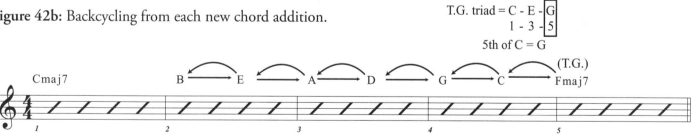

**Note:** To find the 5th of any temporary goal chord without consulting the cycle diagram, simply spell out the T.G. triad and choose the last note. For example, if F is the T.G. and the F triad is spelled F–A–C, C is the 5th and resolves to F.

* "Odd" because chord progressions tend to to be in two-measure phrases. So a two-bar chord pattern would "resolve" on bar 3 – an "odd" measure.

Chord qualities for the root tones in a cycle may be major, minor, or dominant. They are most often seen as either a sequence of consecutive dominant 7th chords (B7–E7–A7–D7) or one or more minor 7th chords followed by one or more dominant 7th chords (Am7–D7–G; or Bm7(♭5)–E7–Am7–D7–G; or Bm7(♭5)–Em7–A7–D7–G, etc.). My choice of quality and embellishment for Example 42c is somewhat arbitrary since there is no melody present.

**Figure 42c:** Chord additions with chord qualities.

**Example 65:** The melody and chord progression from the first five measures of "My Foolish Heart." Play, sing or whistle the melody.

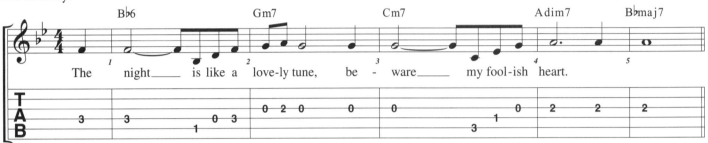

Figures 43–47 show a process I generally use for experimenting with backcycling, tritone substitution, and substitution with relative and secondary relative minors. My selection of chord qualities and embellishments was informed by the melody and chosen by ear. Always play, sing or whistle the melody.

**Figure 43:** Backcycling from measure 3 (temporary goal = Cm7) produced Dm9–G7. The G7(♯5) in measure 2 worked well with the melody as a re-harmonization for the original Gm7.

**Figure 44:** Backcycling from measure 5 produced Cm7–F7 (iim7–V7 of B♭maj7) which actually sounded less interesting to me than the original Adim7 in measure 4! (Not all change is good.)

**Figures 45 and 46:** Searching for other possible substitutions for B♭maj7, in measure 5, I tried the relative and secondary relative minors of B♭maj7 (Gm7 and Dm7) to serve as temporary goal chords from which to backcycle. Backcycling from Gm7 produced Am7–D7(♭5) in measure 4. Backcycling from Dm7 produced Em9–A7. One of these works, the other does not. Before going further, test both these possibilities and see which one you would choose. Be sure to sing the melody as you make your choice.

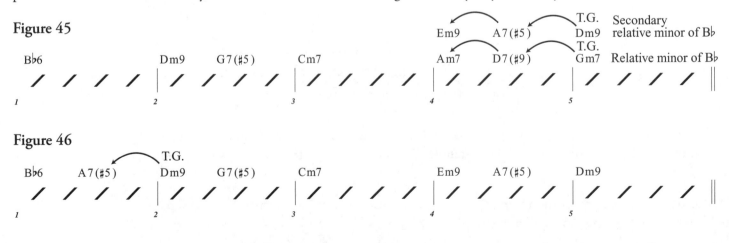

Following, in Figure 47 and then in Example 65, are my choices of substitutions and additions for the first five measures of "My Foolish Heart."

**Figure 47**

**Example 65**

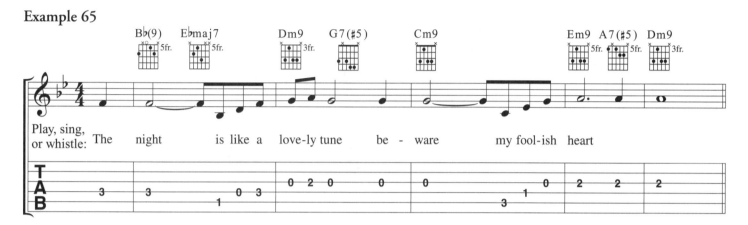

The following complete arrangement "My Foolish Heart" includes all the approaches to chord substitution and addition outlined in this chapter. Below is a measure by measure summary of these approaches for your analysis.

Measure 1: Ebmaj9 is a tritone sub for A7 chord, and the A7 is produced by backcycling from Dm9.

Measure 2: Dm11–G7 is the result of backcycling from the Cm9 in measure 3.

Measure 4: Em11–A7 is the result of backcycling from Dm9 in measure 5.

Measure 5: Dm9 is the secondary relative minor sub for the original Bbmaj7. The D7(#9) is a chord addition resulting from backcycling from the Gm7 in measure 6.

Measure 6: Db9 is a chord addition by chromatic approach to Cm9 in measure 7.

Measure 8: C13 is the result of backcycling from the original F7.

Measure 9: The Bbmaj7 is the relative major sub for the original Gm7.

Measure 10: E9 is the tritone of Bb13. It is also a chromatic approach chord to the Eb6 in measure 11.

Measure 11: Cm7 is a chord addition derived from the relative minor of Eb major.

Measure 15: Dm7 is the relative minor sub for the original Fmaj7; and G13 is the result of backcycling from the Cm7 in measure 16. The Dbm7 is the tritone sub for G13.

Measure 16: Cm7 is the minor 7th sub for the original F7. It also could be seen as the result of backcycling from F7(b13).

Measure 20: Eb9(#11) is the tritone sub for the original Adim7.

Measure 26: Ebm9–Ab9—the melodic common tone substitution for Gb13 (melody note Bb). The F#7–G7 are both chromatic approach chords to Ab7.

Measure 27: Ab13(#11) is the melodic common tone addition for the original Bbmaj7.

Measure 28: Abmaj7 is the tritone of the original Dm7(b5). The Db chord is the tritone sub for the original G7.

Measure 30: Cm11 is the minor 7 from the 5th of F7. It is also the result of backcycling from F7. The G13 comes from backcycling from Cm7 and the Ab13 is a chromatic approach chord sub for the original F7.

Measure 31: Bmaj13 is the melodic common tone sub for original Bbmaj7 also a chromatic approach chord for Bb(9) in measure 32.

# MY FOOLISH HEART

Words by NED WASHINGTON
Music by VICTOR YOUNG
*Arranged by*
*HOWARD MORGEN*

# Guide List for Chapter 9

See the Master Guide List at the end of the book for publisher and item number information for each book.

### *Creative Chord Substitution for Jazz Guitar,* Eddie Arkin
This book contains complete, finely detailed discussions and demonstrations of chord substitution and chord addition including all the techniques discussed in this book and lots more! Author Eddie Arkin suggests in the book's forward that you pay special attention to the first three chapters, "whether you know the stuff or not," to thoroughly assimilate the foundations for the advanced concepts that follow. (Essential reading for upper intermediate to advanced players.)

### *Chord Chemistry,* Ted Greene
Concepts and techniques for chord substitution, pages 58–165.
Substitutions applied to chord-melody treatment of "Greensleeves," pages 176–179.

### *Concepts: Arranging for Fingerstyle Guitar,* Howard Morgen
Techniques for substitution and addition applied to "Greensleeves," pages 72–97.

### *Howard Morgen's Solo Guitar (Insights, Arranging Techniques & Classic Jazz Standards)*
Substitution and addition techniques discussed and applied to "Oh Susanna," pages 117–129.

### *Solo Jazz Guitar Method,* Barry Greene
Chord movement, major and minor clichés, three-note voicings, pages 25–27. Advanced methods of harmonization, pages 30–36.

# Chapter 10: Natural Harmonics

There are two types of harmonics produced on guitar: **natural and artificial.** Natural harmonics are chime-like tones produced by lightly touching a vibrating string at certain points along its length called *nodes.* Harmonics in standard notation are notated on the staff with diamond-shaped noteheads. In TAB, harmonics are indicated by fret numbers enclosed within open diamond shapes. See Example 67.

**Example 67**

B harmonic sounded on the 2nd string, 12th fret

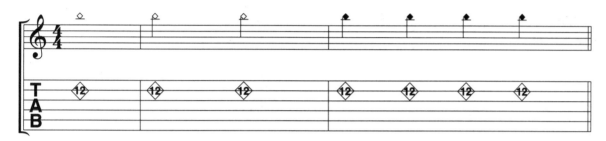

## How to Produce Natural Harmonics

> Step 1: Lightly touch the 2nd string directly over (not behind) the 12th fret with the tip of a fretting-hand finger. Do not depress the string; just touch it.

> Step 2: Sound the 2nd string with your thumb or pick and instantly lift your fingertip, allowing the string to vibrate freely.

Precise coordination between both hands is essential. If you allow your fingertip to remain on the string after it's sounded, or if you lift it before you strike the string, the harmonic will not sound.

The natural harmonics that provide the greatest volume and clarity of tone and pitch are located across all six strings at the 12th fret. See Example 68.

In standard notation, a natural harmonic at the 12th fret produces the same pitch, and is notated in the same position on the staff, as it would if the string were depressed at that fret.

**Example 68**

Natural harmonics, 12th fret

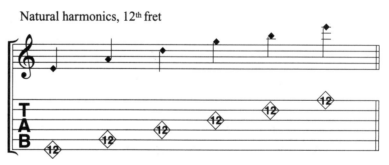

Next in terms of degree of volume, clarity of tone, and pitch are the natural harmonics produced at the 7th and 5th frets respectively. See Examples 69 and 70.

**Example 69**

Natural harmonics, 7th fret

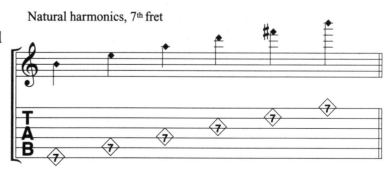

A natural harmonic sounded at the 7th fret shares the same letter name as its fretted-note counterpart but sounds and is notated one octave higher. See Example 69.

Natural harmonics sounded at the 5th fret do not share the same letter name as regular notes played on the same string and fret. They produce tones two octaves higher than the open strings on which they are located or one octave higher than the octave harmonics located on the same string at the 12th fret. The 5th fret harmonic produces a note an octave and a 5th higher than the fretted note. See Example 70.

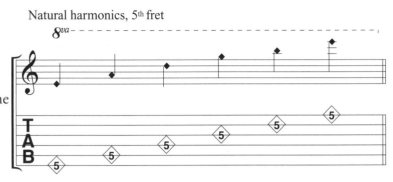

**Example 70**

Natural harmonics, 5th fret

Other natural harmonics are available across all six strings at the 3rd, 4th, 9th, and 16th frets but they are much more difficult to produce, weaker in volume, and are of uneven and lesser tone quality.

Natural harmonics at the 4th fret are produced by placing a fretting-hand finger slightly to the left of the 4th fret. They sound two octaves higher than fretted notes at the same position. The imperfect natural harmonics produced slightly to the right of the 3rd fret sound one octave higher than the harmonics produced at the 7th fret.

## Plucking-Hand Harmonic Technique

Natural harmonics can also be produced using a fingerstyle technique that involves only the plucking hand without the aid of the fretting hand. Although usually only employed for natural harmonics located above the 12th fret (frets 16, 19, and 24), this important technique, used in conjunction with fretted notes, is essential for the production of artificial harmonics (see Chapter 11).

**Example 71**

Example 71 demonstrates sounding a natural harmonic E on the 2nd fret of the 1st string with plucking-hand technique. Use your index finger to touch the "node" point (12th fret) and pluck the string with your ring finger (see steps below).

Step 1: Point with the index finger (*i*) of your plucking hand held as straight as possible and *lightly* touch the 1st string with the fleshy part of your fingertip directly over the 12th node.

Step 2: As you "touch down" with your index fingertip sound the 1st string with either your ring finger (*a*), your thumb (*p*), or possibly your little finger (*c*); then immediately withdraw your index finger from the string, allowing it to vibrate freely. As with two-handed production of natural harmonics, precise coordination is essential in producing a clear, bell-like harmonic. Now apply this technique to the remaining five strings at the 12th fret.

Play Exercise 10 using plucking-hand technique.

**Exercise 10**

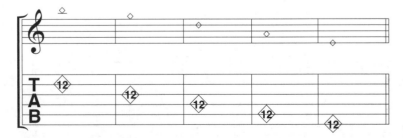

None of the remaining material in this chapter requires the use of plucking-hand harmonic technique since there are no natural harmonics employed above the 12th fret and no artificial harmonics are present. Plucking-hand harmonic technique is used extensively with artificial harmonics in Chapter 11.

**Exercise 11:** An exercise with natural harmonics.

**Example 72:** The first two measures from "'Round Midnight" with natural harmonics.

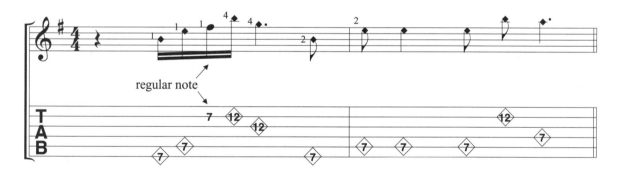

**Example 72a**

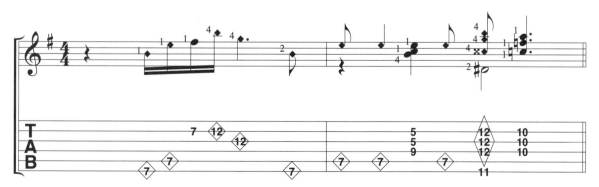

# 'ROUND MIDNIGHT

Words by
BERNIE HANIGHEN
Music by
COOTIE WILLIAMS and THELONIOUS MONK
*Arranged by*
*HOWARD MORGEN*

**Slowly, rubato**
*Intro:*

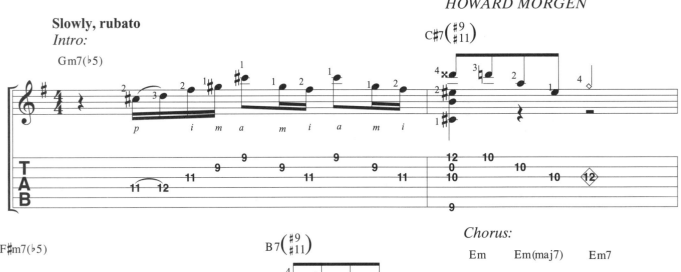

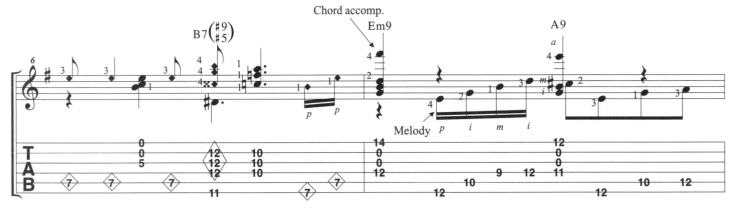

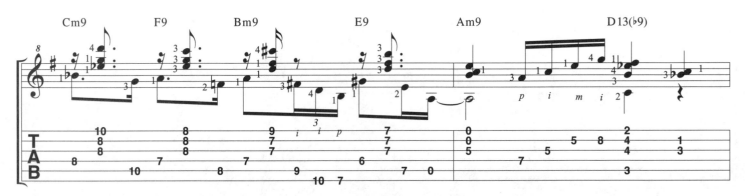

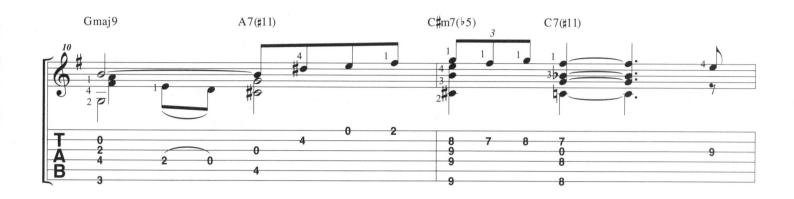

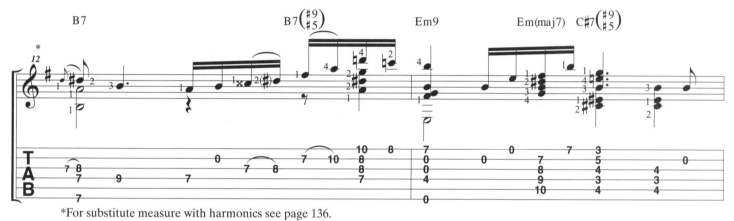

*For substitute measure with harmonics see page 136.

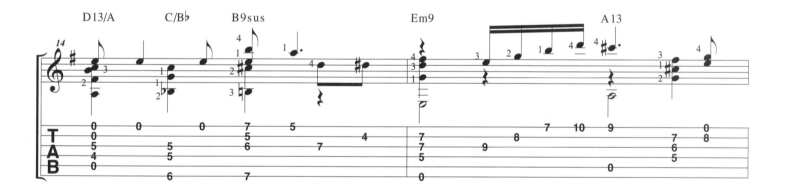

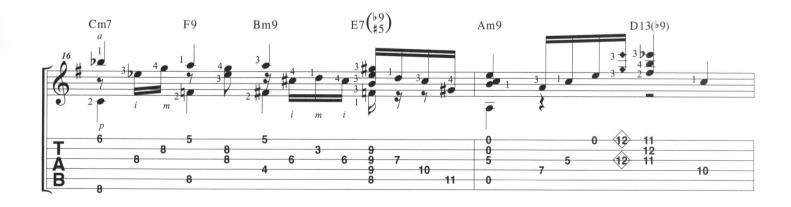

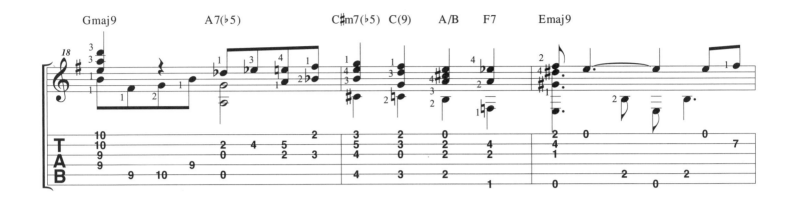

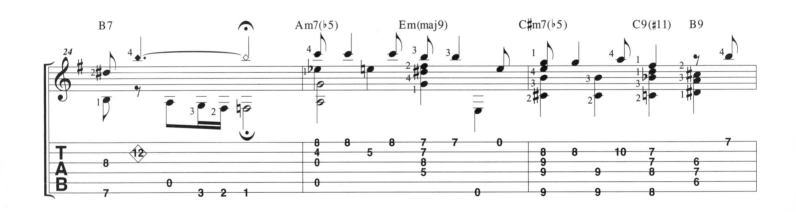

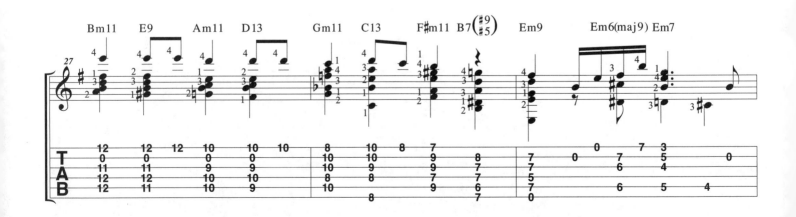

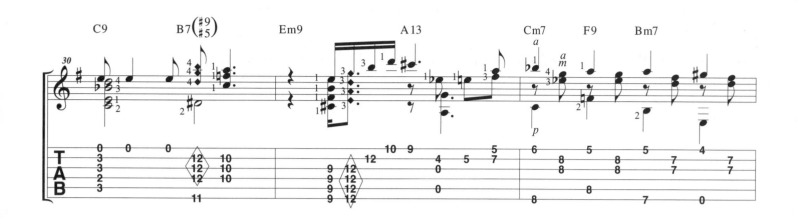

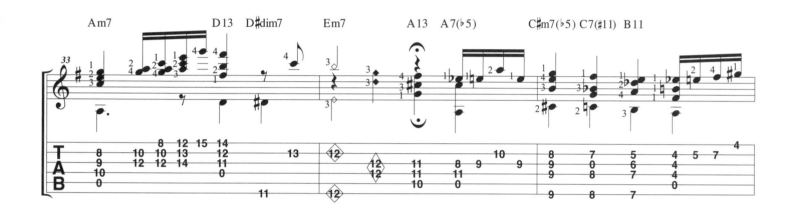

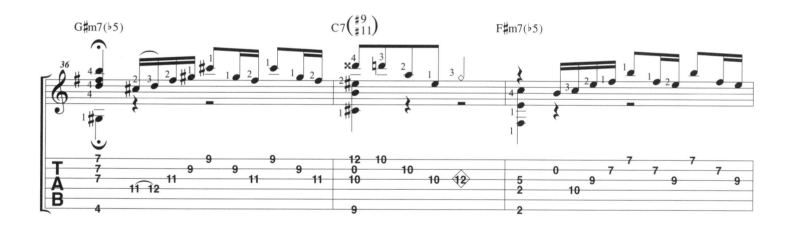

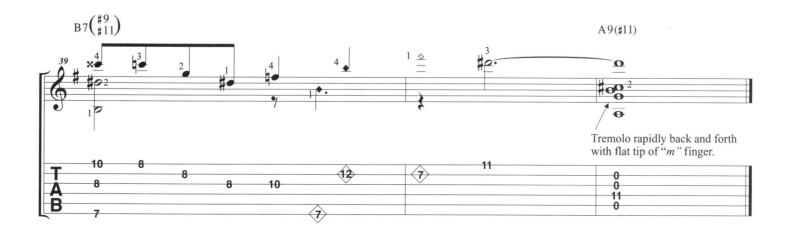

Tremolo rapidly back and forth with flat tip of "*m*" finger.

# Guide List for Chapter 10

See the Master Guide List at the end of the book for publisher and item number information for each book.

*Howard Morgen's Solo Guitar (Insights, Arranging Techniques & Classic Jazz Standards)*
Incorporating natural harmonics and regular fretted notes, pages 55–57.
"Invitation," pages 58–63.

# Chapter 11:
# Artificial Harmonics

## Plucking-Hand Harmonic Technique to Produce Artificial Harmonics

Plucking-hand harmonic technique (Chapter 10) makes it possible to produce pure, bell-like artificial harmonics of equal value and tone quality for any note regardless of its location on the fingerboard. Artificial harmonics sound, and are notated, one octave higher than their fretted counterparts. They are produced by maintaining a distance of 12 frets between the fretted note and the node point at which the artificial harmonic is sounded.

The node point for any given fretted note is always 12 frets higher than the fretted note. In effect, each fretted note becomes a new "nut" with a potential node that can produce an octave harmonic located exactly 12 frets higher on the same string. For example, sound a natural harmonic B on the 2nd string at the 12th fret with plucking-hand harmonic technique.

Now, if you depress C (2nd string, 1st fret) the node at which your plucking hand can produce an artificial C octave harmonic will now be located above the 13th fret, 2nd string (12 + 1 = 13).

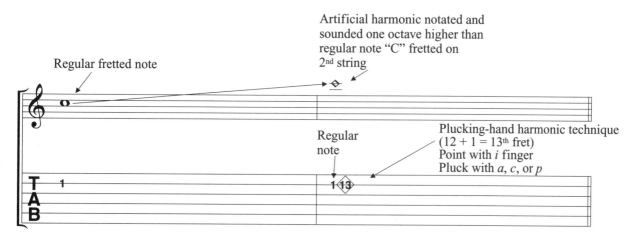

With fretted tones C♯ and D:

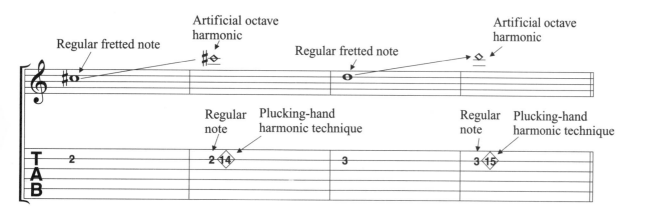

Excerpt from "My Funny Valentine" (no harmonics).

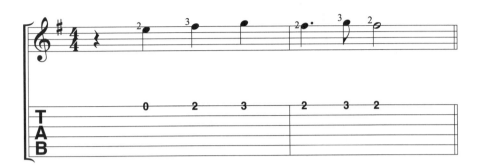

The same excerpt from "My Funny Valentine" with natural and artificial octave harmonics using plucking-hand harmonic technique. (Remember to point to node with index finger and pluck with ring finger or thumb.)

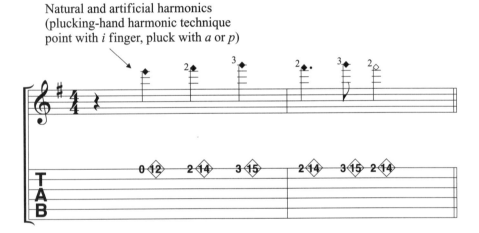

Now let's add bass notes. Point to the node with your index finger, pluck the harmonic with your ring finger and the bass notes with your thumb. (Note adjustment of fretting hand fingering to accommodate the bass notes.)

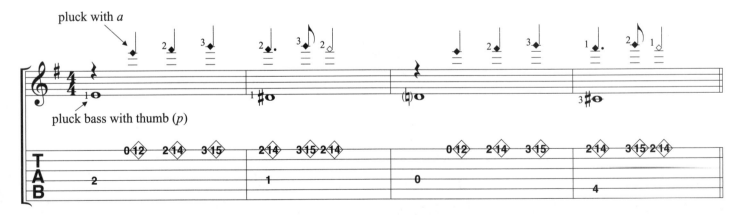

**Exercise 12:** This is a C major scale with natural and artificial harmonics. Again, touch the node point with you index finger and pluck with either your ring finger or thumb. (**Note:** As you've already seen, plucking with the ring finger allows you to use your thumb to play bass notes.)

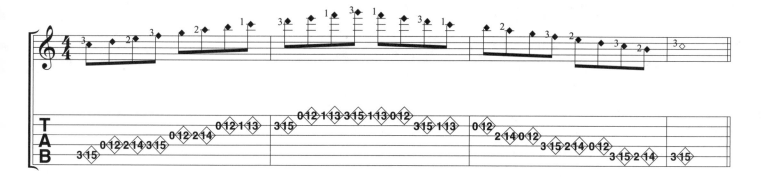

Using artificial harmonics to "trace" a chord shape above the 12th fret.

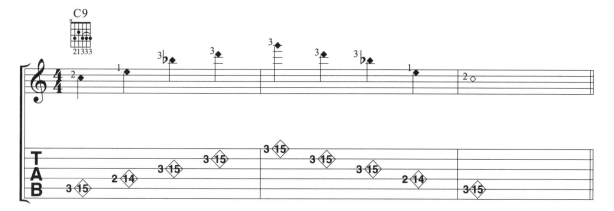

Figure 48 shows, in diagram format, the same C9 chord shape as above, fretted at the 2nd and 3rd frets and sounded by *tracing* the chord shape with plucking-hand harmonic technique exactly 12 frets higher than fretted.

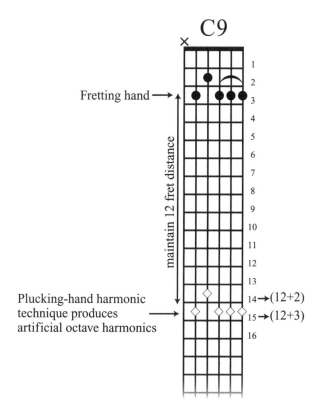

**Example 73:** Combining regular tones on open strings with natural harmonics at the 12<sup>th</sup> fret.

Using the plucking-hand harmonic technique, sound all regular notes with either your ring finger or little finger and sound all harmonics with your thumb while lightly touching the node point with your index finger directly over the 12<sup>th</sup> fret.

Example 73

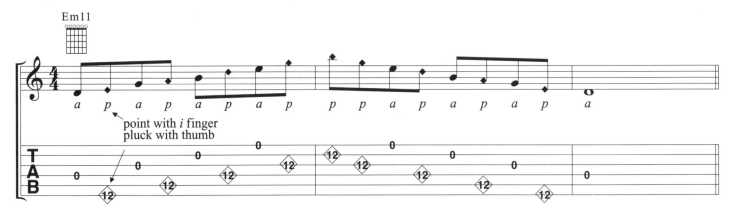

**Example 74:** Combining regular tones with artificial harmonics (Fm11).

Depress the 1<sup>st</sup> finger of your fretting hand across the 1<sup>st</sup> fret. Using plucking-hand harmonic technique, sound all diamond-shaped artificial harmonics with your thumb while lightly touching the node point with your index finger directly over the 13<sup>th</sup> fret.

Example 74

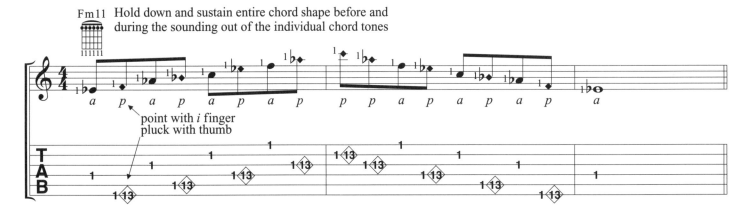

# Combining Natural and Artificial Harmonics with Regular Tones

Natural and artificial harmonics alternated with or sounded simultaneously with regular tones **in the same octave** can deceive the ear into perceiving all the tones as harmonics! Alternating harmonics with regular tones creates an ear-pleasing effect of cascading chime-like tones. A single harmonic sounded in the bass voice simultaneously with one or more regular tones can resemble the sound of an electric piano or steel guitar. (**Note:** Harmonics and regular tones do not have to be strictly alternated to produce a chime-like effect so long as one tone in any combination of three is a harmonic.)

Following are three approaches for sounding a C9<sup>th</sup> chord shape combining regular notes with artificial harmonics. Play each exercise chromatically up the fingerboard.

**Exercise 13:** A single line scale and arpeggio.

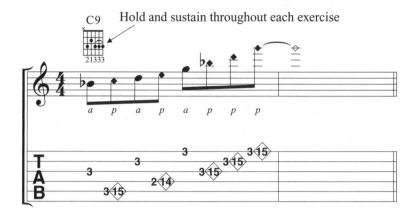

**Exercise 13a:** As major 2$^{nd}$ and minor 3$^{rd}$ intervals. (Although the octave harmonics in this example are higher in pitch then the up-stemmed regular notation above them, they are notated in the bass voice with down-stems to simplify reading.)

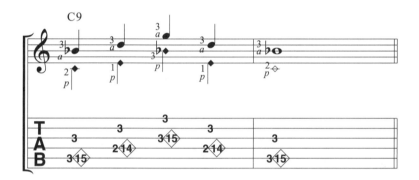

**Exercise 13b:** Placing an artificial harmonic on the lowest voice of a chord shape containing regular tones. (Notice that this technique produces a chord voicing that would be impossible to replicate on guitar without the inclusion of the octave harmonic.)

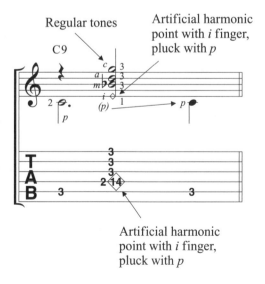

Artificial harmonic
point with *i* finger,
pluck with *p*

**Example 75:** This example combines all three approaches: descending single-line arpeggios, two-note intervals, and the application of a single artificial octave harmonic to the lowest tone of a chord shape.

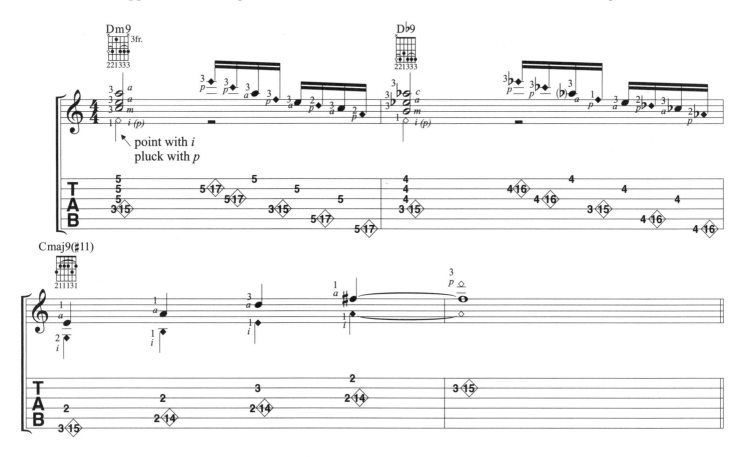

**Example 76:** This example shows the resolution of several different ascending scales and arpeggios: (D9sus to Gmaj7; Eb9sus to Abmaj7; E9sus to Amaj7; and F9sus to Bbmaj7).

**Example 76**

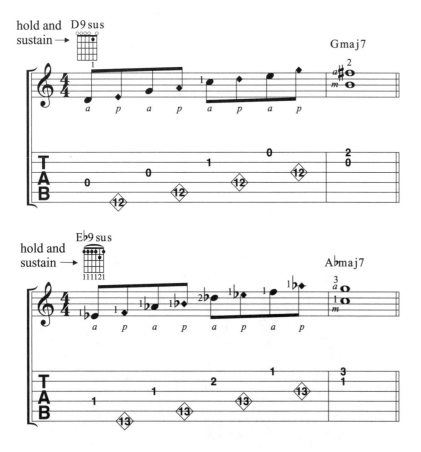

**Example 76 (continued)**

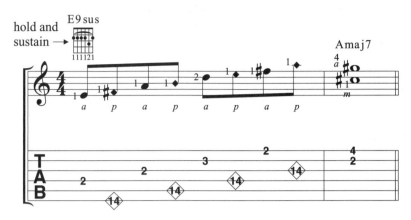

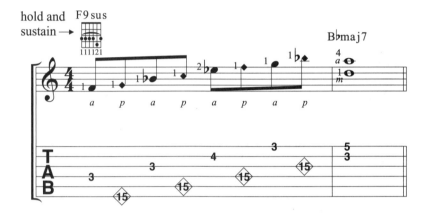

**Example 77:** This is an excerpt from "Speak Low," version no. 2.

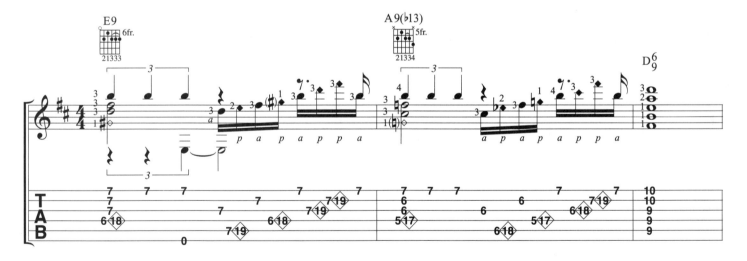

**Example 78:** Suggested replacement (as recorded) from measure 8 of "'Round Midnight."

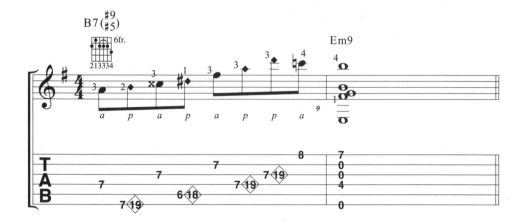

**Example 79:** Excerpt from the closing measures of "Body and Soul," version no. 2.

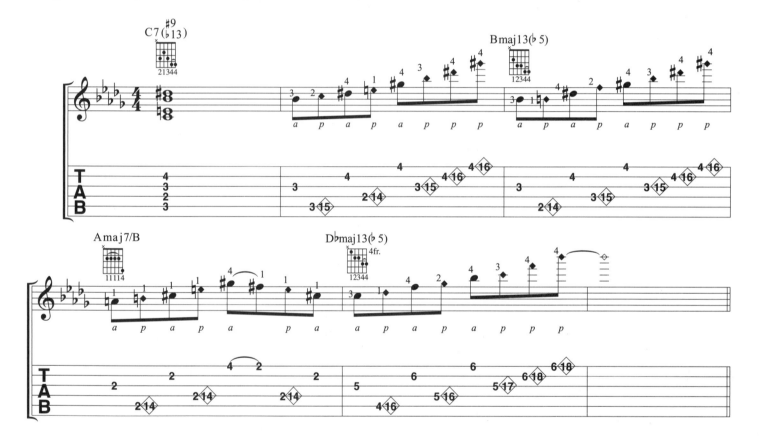

# "Speak Low," version no. 2

This treatment of "Speak Low" features Latin-influenced syncopations in the chord accompaniment. A count is provided to help you with the highly syncopated rhythm. Count aloud and sound the strings where indicated. Strum the introduction and ending entirely with your thumb according to the down (⊓) and up (∨) markings posted above the notation. Play with even eighth notes.

# SPEAK LOW
## (Version 2)

Words by
OGDEN NASH
Music by
KURT WEILL
*Arranged by*
*HOWARD MORGEN*

**With a latin beat**
**(Montuna)**

*Intro:*

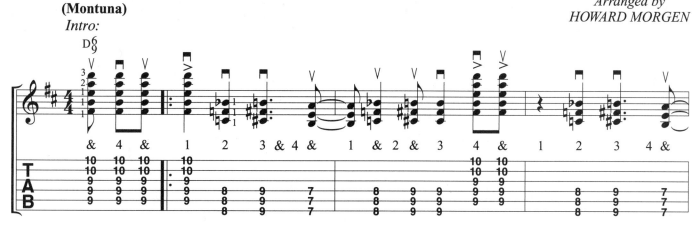

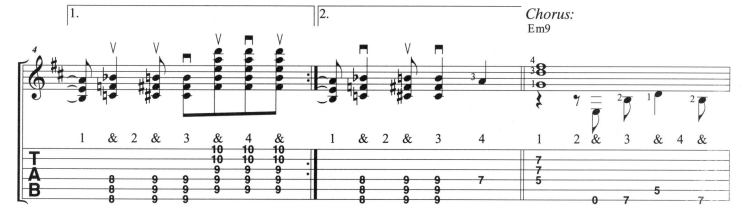

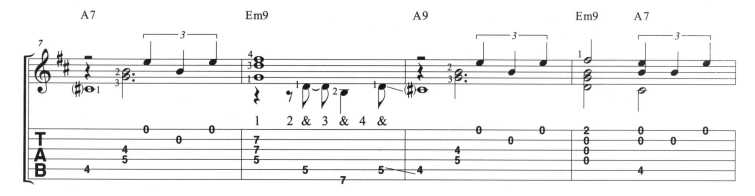

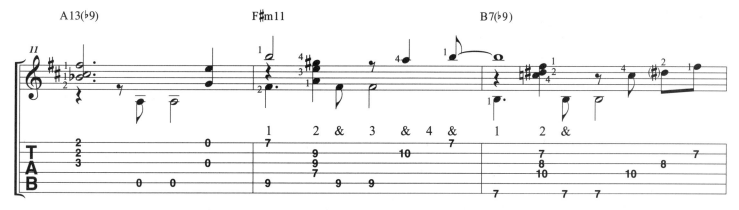

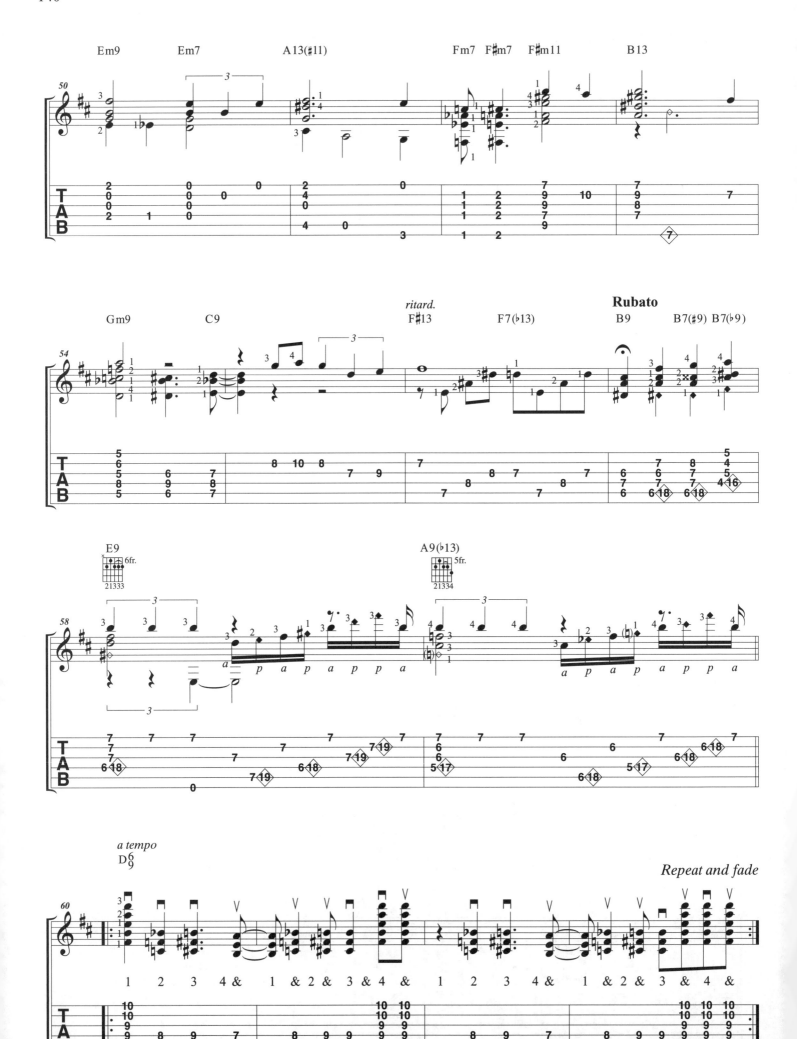

# Guide List for Chapter 11

See the Master Guide List at the end of the book for publisher and item number information for each book.

*Lenny Breau Fingerstyle Jazz*
Combining natural and artificial octave harmonics with regular notes, harp effects, cascades, and chord techniques, pages 23–30.

*"Five O'Clock Bells,"* **Lenny Breau,** pages 31–35.

*" Little Blues,"* **Lenny Breau,** pages 36–48.

*"Freight Train,"* **arranged by Lenny Breau,** pages 49–50.

*Howard Morgen's Solo Guitar (Insights, Arranging Techniques & Classic Jazz Standards)*
Artificial harmonics, pages 64–65.
Techniques, pages 66–69.
*"Misty,"* pages 71-73
*"Laura,"* pages 74-79

# Chapter 12: Drop D Tuning

Lowering the 6th string (E) down a whole step to D is a common variation on standard tuning which permits piano-like voicings that would be impossible to play in standard tuning. Drop D tuning (D–A–D–G–B–E) produces a tone on the open 6th string one octave lower in pitch than D on the open 4th string. Accordingly, all notes on both the 6th and 4th strings share the same fret location. A one octave interval shape is formed by simply barring across the 6th and 4th strings with any finger of the fretting hand.

**Figure 49**

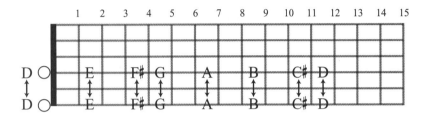

**Figure 50:** Any note located on the 6th string in standard tuning is now located *two frets higher* in Drop D tuning.

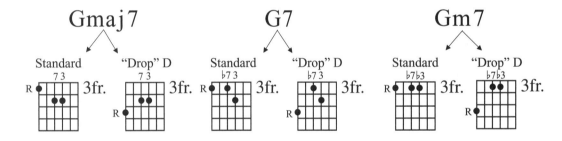

**Figure 51:** Six-string voicings with Drop D tuning producing a variety of interesting sounds mixing open strings with fretted notes.

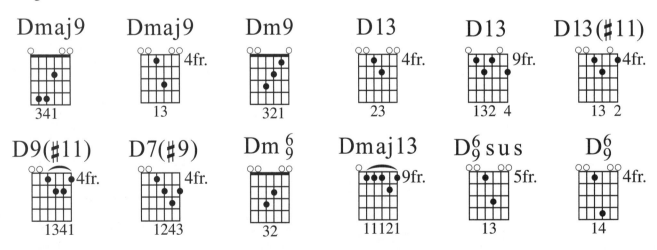

**Figure 52:** The following voicings would not be possible to play on guitar with standard tuning.

**Figure 53:** Drop D voicings for "My Funny Valentine."

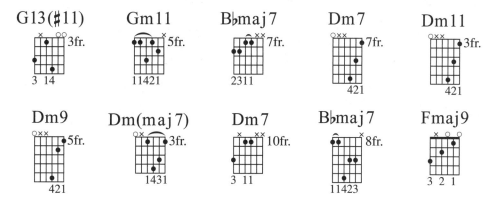

# MY FUNNY VALENTINE
### (Version 2)

Words by
LORENZ HART
Music by
RICHARD RODGERS
*Arranged by*
*HOWARD MORGEN*

"Drop" D
⑥ = D

*See next page for optional ending.

# MY FUNNY VALENTINE
**(Optional Ending as Recorded)**

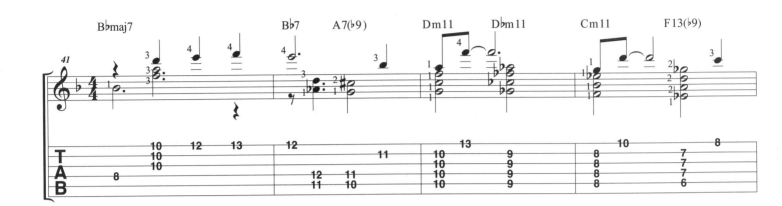

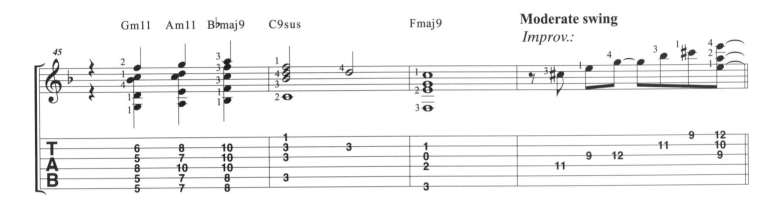

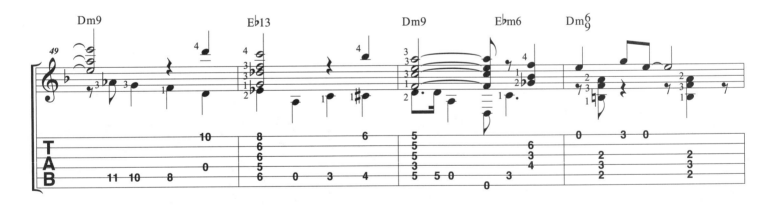

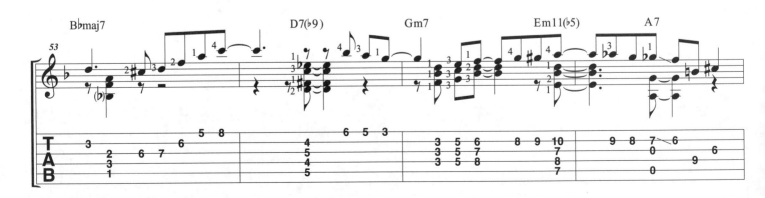

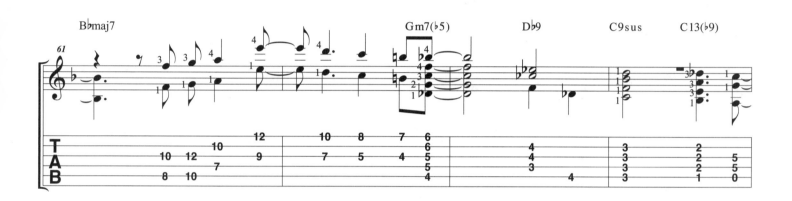

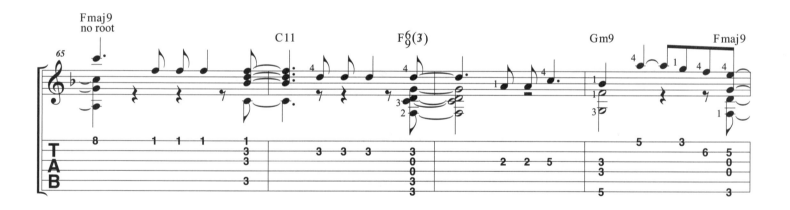

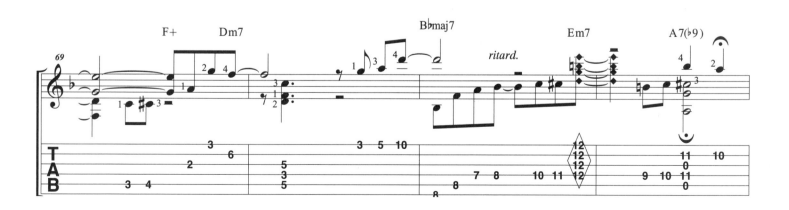

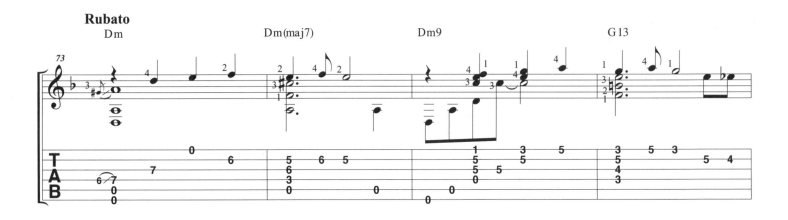

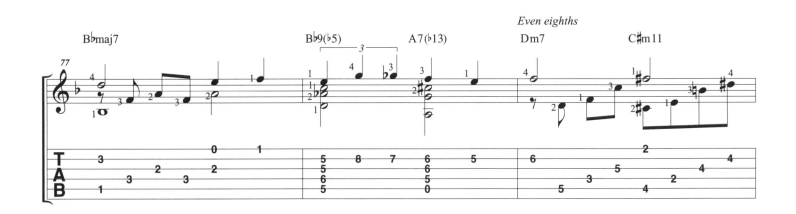

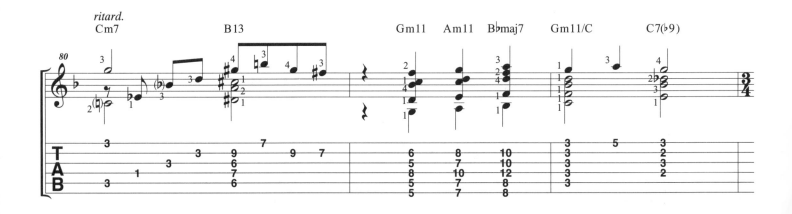

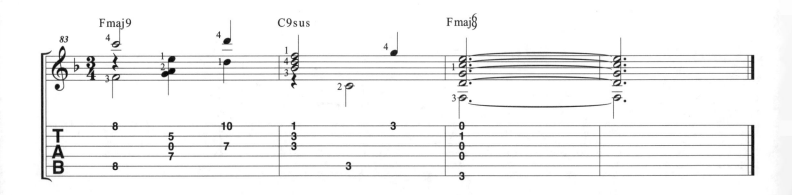

# ALONE TOGETHER
## (Version 2)

Lyrics by
HOWARD DIETZ
Music by
ARTHUR SCHWARTZ
*Arranged by*
*HOWARD MORGEN*

"Drop" D
⑥ = D

**Slowly, freely**

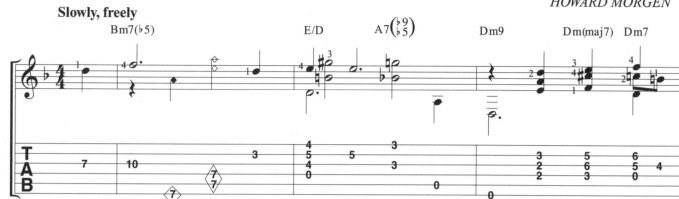

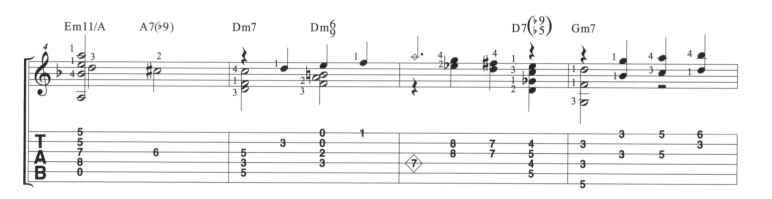

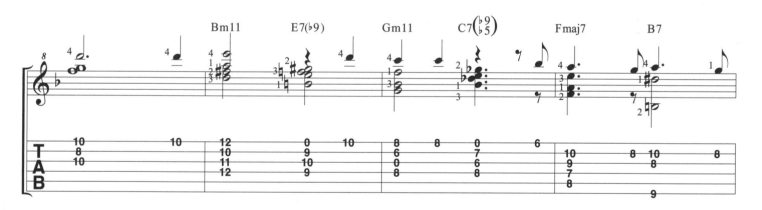

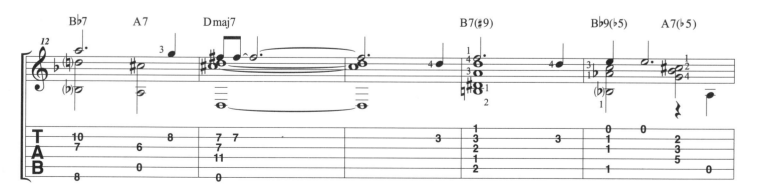

(For optional ending: Jump to Improv. section—measure 49)

*Optional ending: "Improv.", with a moderate strong beat*

# Guide List for Chapter 12

See the Master Guide List at the end of the book for publisher and item number information for each book.

*Concepts: Arranging for Fingerstyle Guitar,* **Howard Morgen**
Low D tuning, page 124.
"The Boy Next Door," pages 126–127.

*The Bill Evans Collection for Solo Guitar,* **Arranged by Greg Stone**
Unique closed jazz piano-like voicings made accessible with a "C" tuning system

*Beyond Basics: Introducing Alternate Tunings for Fingerstyle Guitar,* **Mark Hanson**
Alternate tunings

*Martin Simpson Teaches Alternate Tunings*
Alternate tunings

# Chapter 13:
# Choosing a Key for Your Arrangement

Choice of key is an important early decision that influences the availability of melody and chord tones on the fingerboard as well as the potential for the various approaches to self-accompaniment outlined in Part One. For example, my choice of the key of D major for "The More I See You," version no. 2 made melody notes available on open strings which enabled me to set the entire melody part in the bass voice below the steady, rhythmic chord accompaniment above. This approach would have been difficult, if not impossible, to achieve on guitar in the song's original key of E♭ major (see "The More I See You," version no. 2).

## "Guitar Friendly" Keys

Songs written in A♭, B♭, B, D♭, E♭, and G♭ major and minor are generally more difficult to adapt to the guitar fingerboard with its standard tuning system. For this reason, it's common when arranging for self-accompanied solo guitar to transpose songs written in these keys to the more "guitar friendly" keys of E, A, D, G, C, and F major; and E, A and D minor which contain a high percentage of tones that are available in standard tuning on open strings. Note that this common practice of using "guitar friendly" keys has significant advantages as well as a number of disadvantages that are discussed later in this chapter.

Below is a table of nine guitar friendly keys that illustrates the availability of open strings in each key for use, in conjunction with fretted notes, as bass notes, melody notes, chords and natural harmonics.

The table below shows the guitar friendly keys and the notes in each of those keys. Circled notes can be played on open strings and the F♯ with an asterisk can be played as a natural harmonic—7th fret on the 2nd string.

**Figure 54**

◯ = open strings
* = natural harmonic = 7th fret, 2nd string (F♯)

| E major | Ⓔ | F♯* | G♯ | Ⓐ | Ⓑ | C♯ | D♯ |
|---------|----|-----|-----|----|----|----|----|
| A major | Ⓐ | Ⓑ | C♯ | Ⓓ | Ⓔ | F♯* | G♯ |
| D major | Ⓓ | Ⓔ | F♯* | Ⓖ | Ⓐ | Ⓑ | C♯ |
| E minor | E | F♯* | Ⓖ | Ⓐ | Ⓑ | C | Ⓓ |
| A minor | Ⓐ | Ⓑ | C | Ⓓ | Ⓔ | F | Ⓖ |
| D minor | Ⓓ | Ⓔ | F | Ⓖ | Ⓐ | B♭ | C |
| C major | C | Ⓓ | Ⓔ | F | Ⓖ | Ⓐ | Ⓑ |
| G major | Ⓖ | Ⓐ | Ⓑ | C | Ⓓ | Ⓔ | F♯ |
| F major | F | Ⓖ | Ⓐ | B♭ | C | Ⓓ | Ⓔ |

# Functions for Open Strings in Guitar Friendly Keys

(see the previous Figure 54):

### As bass notes: Low E, A, and D for principle chords:

- I and IV in E major and i and iv in E minor

- I, IV, and V7 in A major and i, iv, and V7 in A minor

- I and V7 in D major and i and V7 in D minor

### Open strings are also available as bass note roots for:

- ii, II7, iii, III7, vi and VI7 in C major

- ii, II7, V7, vi, and VI7 in G major

- iii, III7, vi, VI7, and vii7($\flat$5) in F major

### As melody notes, chords, and natural harmonics:

- The keys of C major, G major, and E minor contain six notes that can be produced as strong natural harmonics on all six strings at the 12th, 7th and 5th frets. D major, E minor and A minor contain five notes. A major, D minor, and F major contain four notes, and F major contains three notes.

- Natural harmonic F$\sharp$ (2nd string, 7th fret) is available as a melody note in E major, E minor, A major, D major, and D minor (see "'Round Midnight").

- The following treatment of "Stardust" illustrates the advantages of incorporating open strings in conjunction with regular fretted notes.

- Employing open strings as bass notes frees the fretting hand for playing anywhere along the neck: Measures 4, 5, 6, 14, 22, 38, 39, 42, 46.

- Position shifts can be smoothly executed by placing an open string on the beat *before* a position shift: Measures 3, 6, 9, 10, 11, 38.

- In addition to contributing chime-like textures natural harmonics, like all notes produced on open strings, can be used to sustain tones while freeing the fretting hand for playing anywhere along the neck: Measures 1, 6, 7, 11, 28, 48.

- Unusual piano-like voicings and chord textures impossible to produce using only fretted notes are made available by incorporating open strings and/or natural harmonics into the chord voicing: Measures 9, 19, 50.

# STARDUST
### (Version 2)

Music by
HOAGY CARMICHAEL
Words by
MITCHELL PARISH
*Arranged by*
*HOWARD MORGEN*

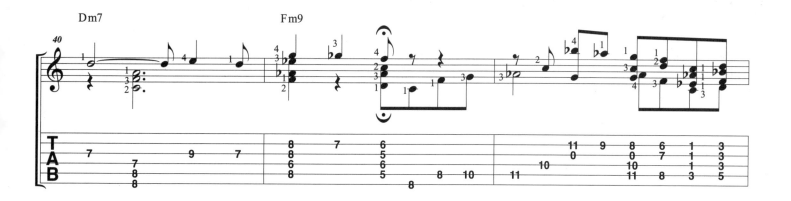

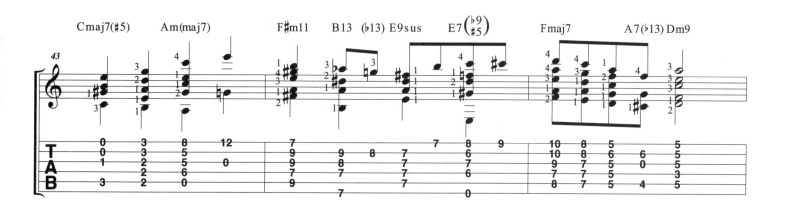

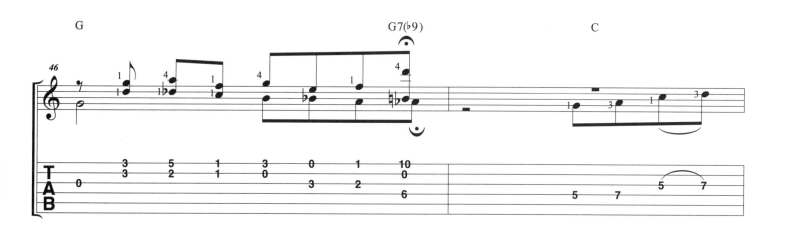

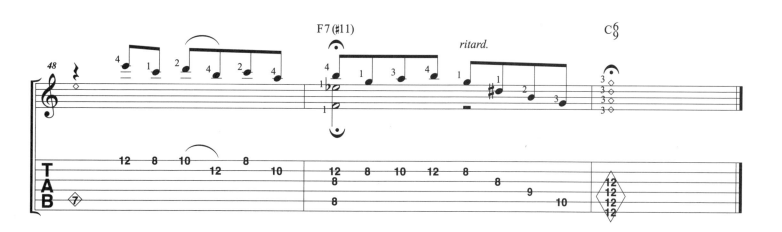

## Alternative Keys vs. Original Keys

While there are many advantages to experimenting with alternative keys, there are also some subtle yet significant disadvantages to consistently avoiding the original keys that happen to be less guitar-friendly. For instance,

- Choosing keys other than the original tends to isolate guitarists from the mainstream of other instrumentalists who are expected and accustomed to playing in original keys.

- Exclusive use of the same few keys throughout a live performance or on solo recordings may result in listener boredom.

- Changing the key may cause a loss of emotional content. This is of less significance in popular music where the key is often changed to accommodate the vocal range of a singer and the song's emotional content resides largely in the singer's interpretation of the lyric.

- Choosing, through patient experimentation, to work within the challenges presented by a less guitar-friendly original key can strengthen your arranging chops and, in the process, you may also uncover some innovative solutions that might never have come to light if you had opted for an alternative key.

## "Body and Soul," version no. 2

"Body and Soul," version no. 2 is a one chorus "improv" that never strays far from the melody. It is set in the original keys of D♭ major and D major. It can be played either as written, straight through to measure 57 or as recorded on track 18, which uses an alternative ending featuring artificial harmonics combined with regular notes beginning on measure 53.

Think of this treatment as a "conversation" with the melody making its statement weaving freely in and out among the middle and bass voices, supported by "answering" comments in the form of melodic and walking bass lines, pedal tones and syncopated chord punctuations.

# BODY AND SOUL
## (Version 2, An "Improv.")

Words by
EDWARD HEYMAN,
ROBERT SOUR and FRANK EYTON
Music by
JOHN GREEN
*Arranged by*
*HOWARD MORGEN*

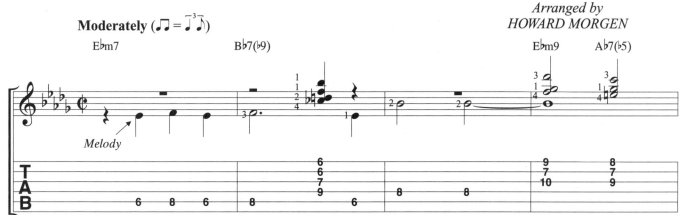

Begin to gradually build to a slow, steady "two" feel groove with swing eighths.

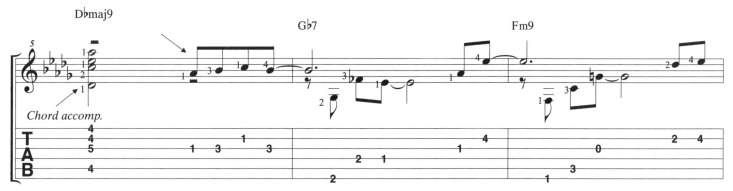

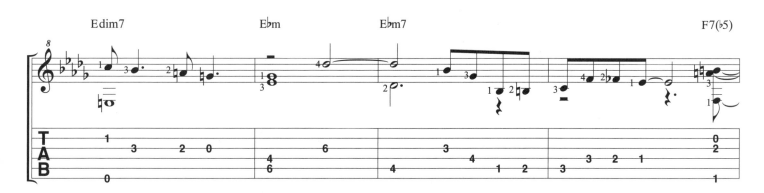

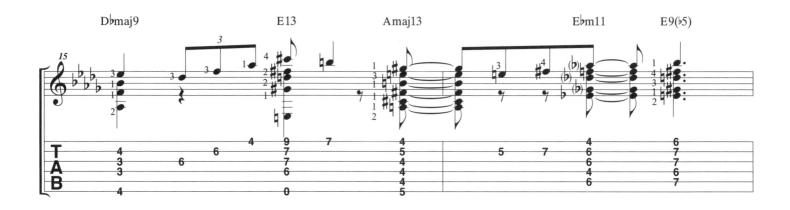

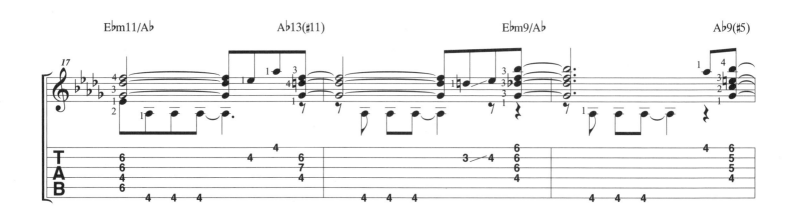

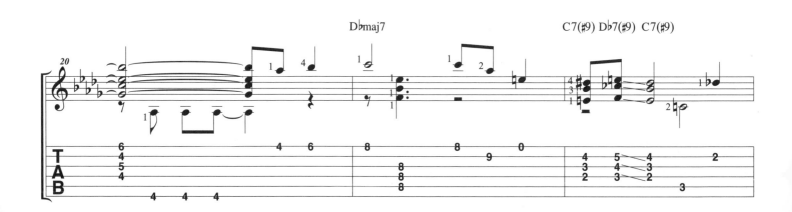

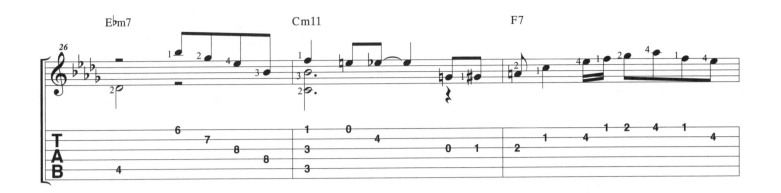

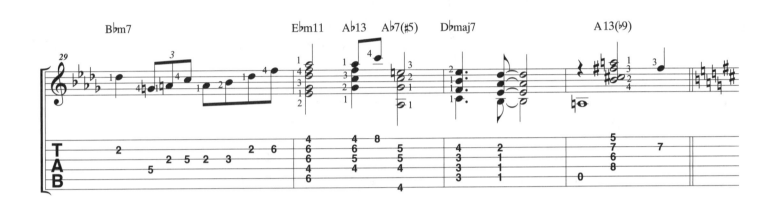

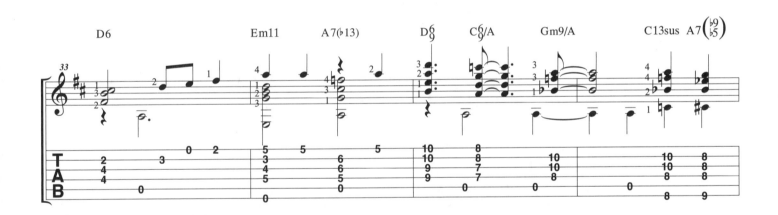

*See next page for optional ending (as recorded).

# BODY AND SOUL
## (Optional Ending as Recorded)

Based on the ideas presented in this chapter, I've listed below some practical suggestions as a general guide when choosing keys for your arrangements.

- Choose original keys for "head" arrangements designed for group interaction.

- When arranging for solo guitar, experiment with both original and alternative keys. Be sure to play through the entire song in each key to spot and remedy potential problem areas. Start with the song's original key and thoroughly investigate all its possibilities before looking further at alternative keys.

- The original keys of many songs may be guitar friendly to begin with (see "Stardust," version no. 2), and even the more difficult original keys will contain opportunities for incorporating open strings and natural or artificial harmonics if you take the time to look for them (see "My Foolish Heart").

- Always sequence both key choices and tempos for variety and pacing in live performances and on solo recordings.

## Guide List for Chapter 13

See the Master Guide List at the end of the book for publisher and item number information for each book.

*Concepts: Arranging for Fingerstyle Guitar,* **Howard Morgen**

# Chapter 14:
# Changing Keys (Modulation)

Key changes can be either **prepared,** or **abrupt**—with little or no transitional material between the old and the new keys. In popular music, key changes are often abrupt, usually occurring at the start of a new chorus and are anticipated by a short sequence of one or more chords leading to the new destination key. An example of this is the well-known treatment of "Mack the Knife," popularized by Bobby Darin and Louis Armstrong, in which each successive new chorus is sung and/or played one semi-tone higher than the previous chorus.

**Example 80:** This excerpt from "It's Only a Paper Moon" shows an abrupt, one-measure key change from C major to D♭ major.

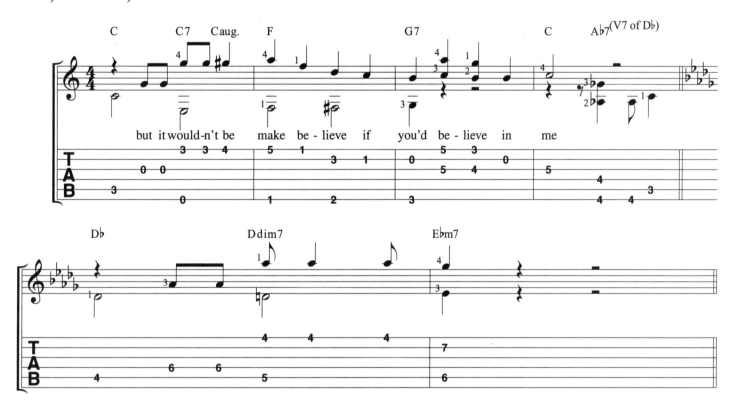

## Transition Chord Sequences

In this brief introduction to the topic of modulation we will focus on three basic chord sequences for introducing abrupt one- or two-measure modulations:

- Major and minor keys can be introduced by the V7 of the new key.

- Major keys can be introduced with a ii7–V7 of the new key.

- Minor keys can be introduced with a ii7(♭5)–V7 of the new key.

All of the above sequences may be embellished depending, as always, on the melody part. In the following four examples, notice how short melodic phrases and good voice leading techniques help carry the ear through the chord changes to the new destination keys.

**Example 81:** "My Foolish Heart" excerpt ending in B♭ major.

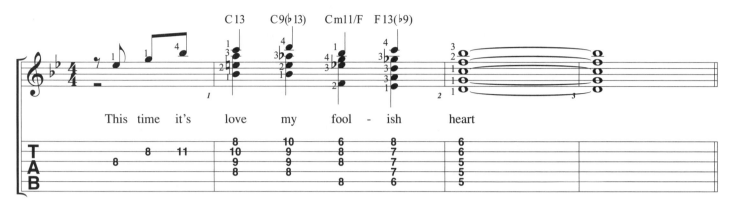

**Example 81a:** Modulating from B♭ major to B major as a destination key. Note the chromatically descending melody line on 2nd string (see TAB) and the use of backcycling to produce a ii7–V7–I into B major: ii7–V7–I: C♯m7–F♯7–Bmaj7.

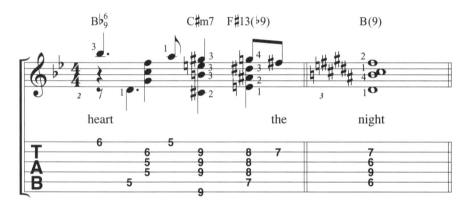

**Example 81b:** Modulating from B♭ major to C major (destination key). Backcycling from C produces the G7. The B♭ melody note moves chromatically up to B♮ (3rd of G7).

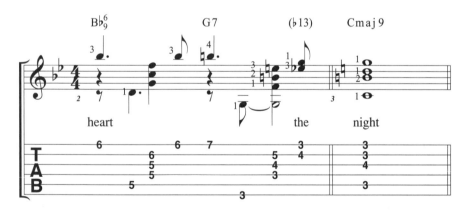

**Example 81c:** Modulation from B♭ major to D♭ major (destination key). Backcycling from the D♭ destination produces: E♭m9 – A♭7 (ii7 – V7 of D♭). The common-tone melody note B♭ becomes the 5th of E♭m9 (ii7 of destination key of D♭ major).

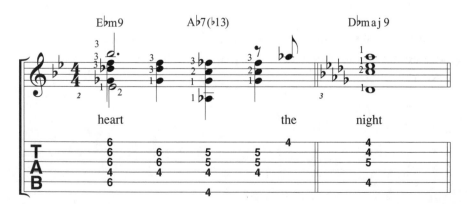

**Example 81d:** Modulation from B♭ major to D major (destination key). Backcycling from D♭maj9 produces: Em7–A7 (ii7–V7 in D).

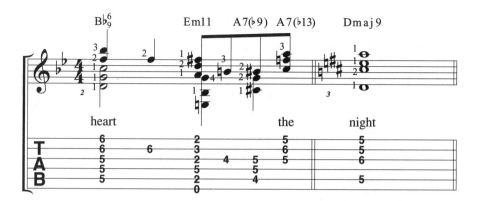

## Modulation Exercises

### Exercise 14

Using either ii7–V7 or V7 of the destination key, try your own one measure modulations from B♭ major to each of the remaining seven keys of: E♭, E, F, G♭, G, A♭, and A major. Begin each new modulation with the same pickup, melody, and chord progression as in measure one of Example 81. All the modulations should start at measure 2 and reach their destination key at measure 3. Here are the ii7–V7 changes for each new key. Embellish to taste:

- Fm7–B♭7–E♭
- F♯m7–B7–E
- Gm7–C7–F
- A♭m7–D♭7–G♭
- Am7–D7–G
- B♭m7–E♭7–A♭
- Bm7–E7–A

The success of your modulations will depend on how well your short, melodic phrases lead the listener's ear to the destination key. I suggest you play straight through the changes as you build your melody lines and let your ear be your guide. After you've completed the exercises, check your completed examples with mine as shown in the following.

Here are my solutions for modulations to E♭, E, F, G♭, G, A♭, and A major (all from B♭).

**Example 81e:** Modulation from B♭ to E♭.

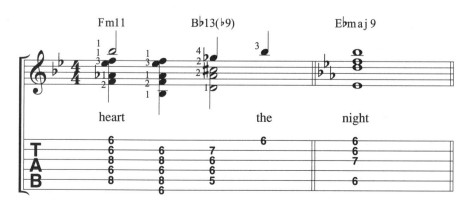

**Example 81f:** Modulation from B♭ to E.

**Example 81g:** Modulation from B♭ to F.

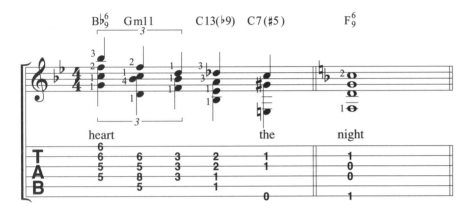

**Example 81h:** Modulation from B♭ to G♭.

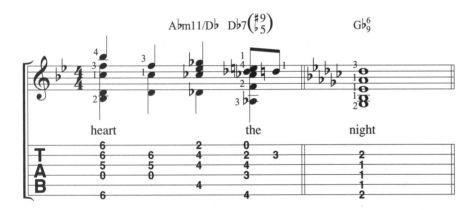

**Example 81i:** Modulation from B♭ to G.

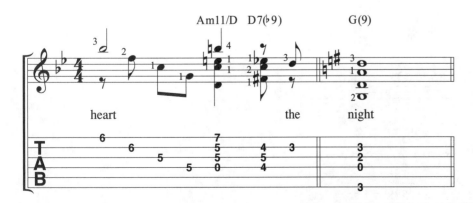

**Example 81j:** Modulation from B♭ to A♭.

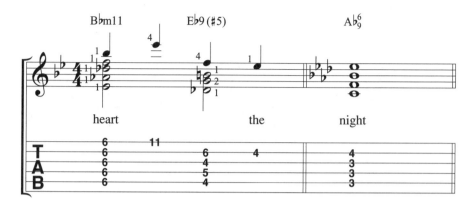

**Example 81k:** Modulation from B♭ to A.

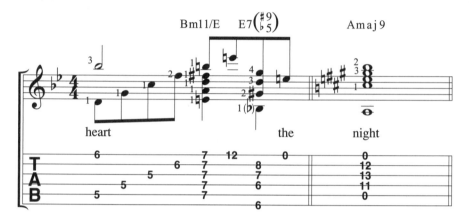

Songs do not always start on the tonic major or tonic minor. For example, "Speak Low" (original key F major), starts on the ii7 chord (Gm7). When making a one-measure modulation to a song that starts on any chord **other than the tonic**, think of the starting chord as **temporary I chord** from which to backcycle.

**Example 82:** A one-measure modulation from the ending of "Speak Low" in F major, modulating to the key of C major. Note that the starting chord in the key of C major is Dm7. A common, and usually effective, sequence of chords for back-cycling from a ii7 chord is ii7(♭5)–V7 (making the ii7 chord the temporary destination key).

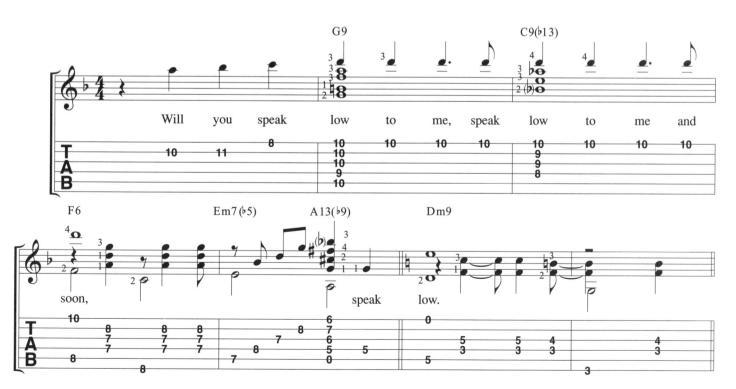

# Three Exercises Modulating to Temporary Tonic

**Exercise 15:** The ending of "Speak Low" in F major, modulating to D major. Starts on ii7 (Em7).
Fill in measures 4–6:

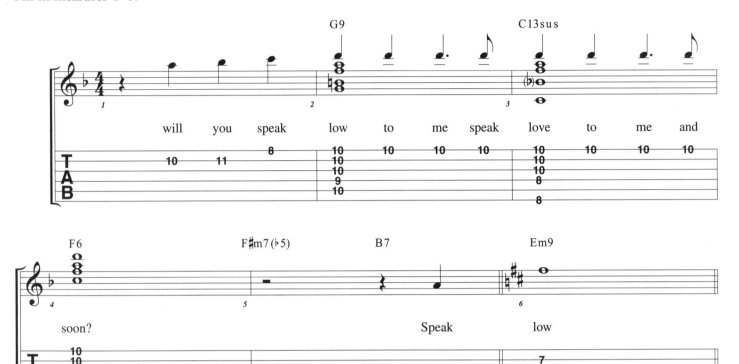

**Exercise 16:** The ending of "Li'l Darlin'" in F major, modulating to G major. Starts on II7 (A7).
Fill in measures 3–5:

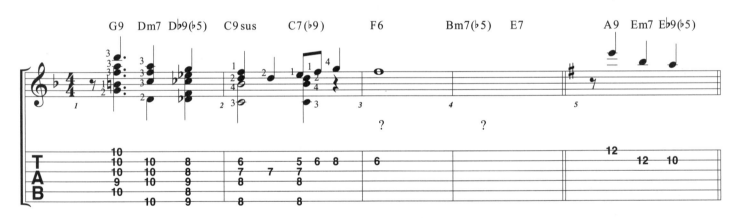

**Exercise 17:** The ending of "My Funny Valentine" in E♭ major, modulating to F major. Starts on vi
(Dm). Fill in measures 4–6:

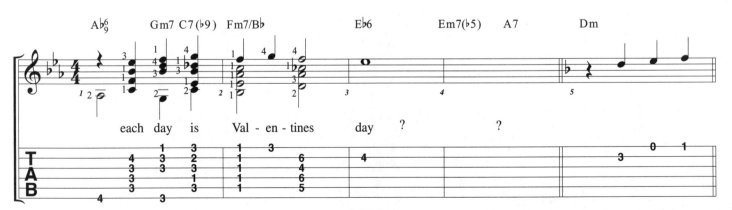

When completed, compare your modulations to mine. My solutions for Exercises 15–17 are presented below in Examples 83–85.

**Example 83:** Modulation from F major to D major (Exercise 15).

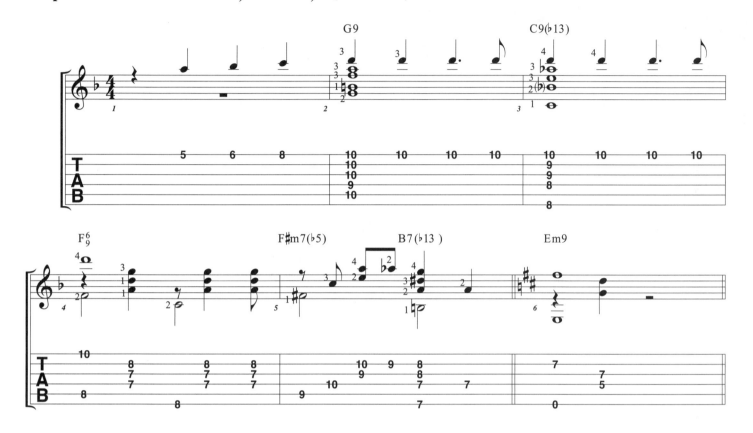

**Example 84:** Modulation from F major to G major (Exercise 16).

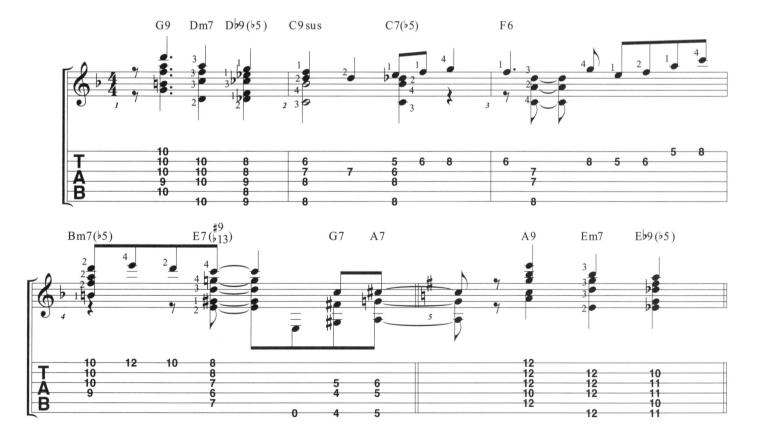

**Example 85:** Modulation from E♭ major to D minor (Exercise 17)

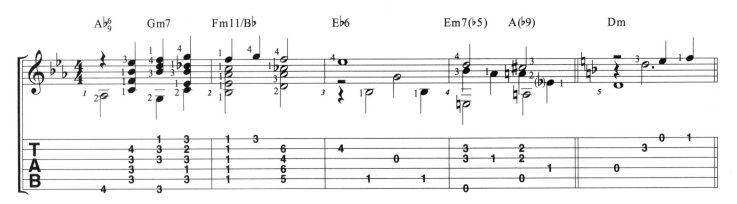

# "The More I See You," version no. 3

Combining ideas from versions 1 and 2 with the addition of a key change.

This treatment features all the approaches to self-accompaniment demonstrated in Part 1, including: block chord-melody style, chord-melody derivations, comping below the melody with short syncopated chord fragments, placing the melody in the bass voice below the accompaniment, and walking bass lines.

It also includes many of the reharmonization techniques and other concepts discussed in Part 2, including: chord embellishment and substitution, natural harmonics, mixing open strings with fretted notes, and modulation.

Note: There is a key change from D major to E♭ major (measures 31–34). You know a modulation hasn't "worked" when you have a desire to return to the original key after the modulation has taken place. This can usually be avoided by immediately reinforcing the modulation with harmonic material that can help further establish and solidify the new key in the ear of the listener. For example, after the modulation from D major to E♭ major generated by a B♭11 chord (V7 of E♭) on the last beat of measure 32, the key of E♭ is reinforced at measures 33–34 by a chromatically descending moving line E♭–D–D♭ moving down to C, producing an A♭7 chord which a creates a pleasing "bluesy" effect. A♭7 then moves on down a semi-tone to a Gm7 chord (the secondary relative minor of E♭), firmly establishing the key of E♭ major (measures 34–35).

# THE MORE I SEE YOU
## (Version 3)

Lyrics by
**MACK GORDON**
Music by
**HARRY WARREN**
*Arranged by*
*HOWARD MORGEN*

**Moderate swing**

*Chorus:*

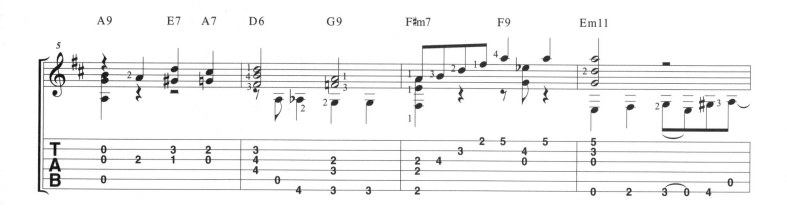

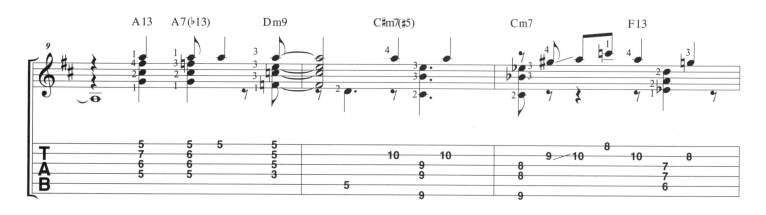

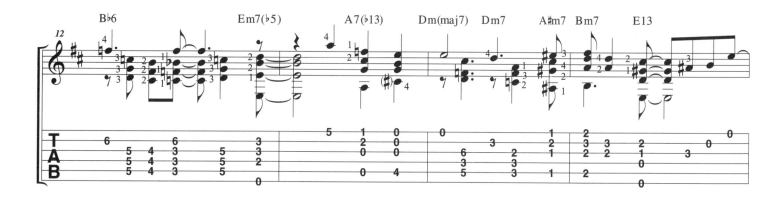

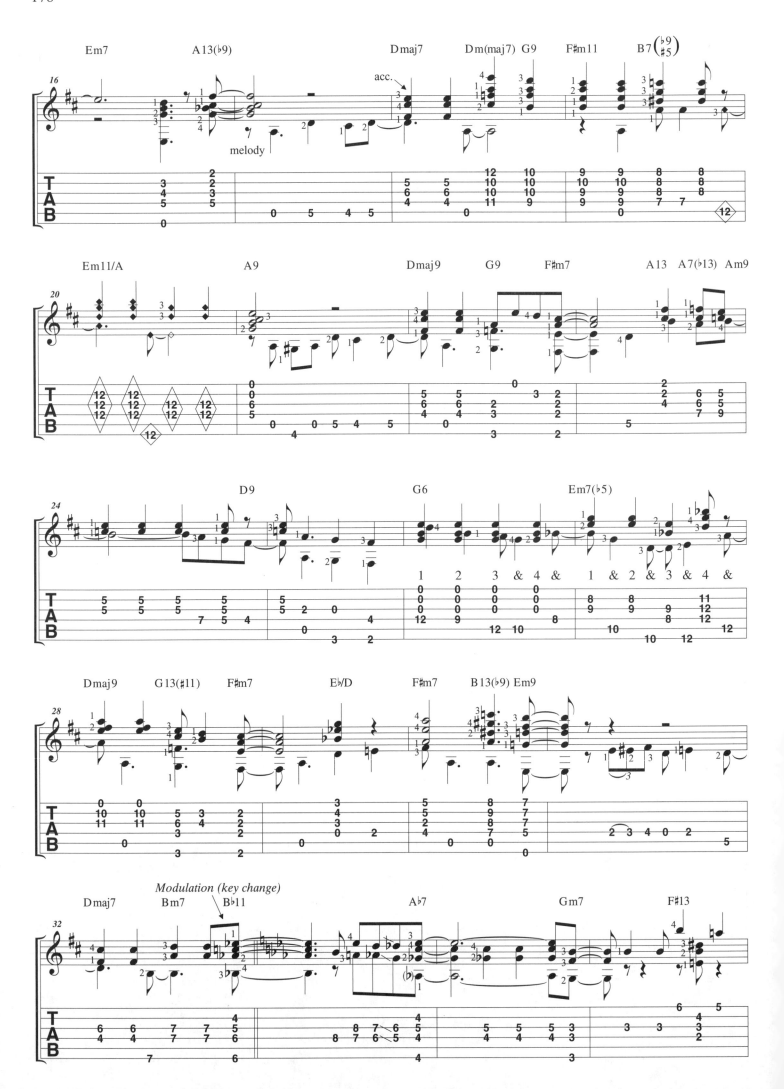

# "It's Only a Paper Moon": Preparatory Exercises with Pedal Tones in the Bass

Playing pedal tones in a fixed syncopated rhythm against a syncopated melody part requires lots of independence between the thumb and fingers of the plucking hand. Measures 28–34 of "It's Only a Paper Moon" make a useful exercise for helping to develop the independence needed to feel the "groove" of this approach.

Here are these measures, isolated for study, together with the timing and finger designation for the fretting hand. All bass note pedal tones on the 6th and 5th strings should be sounded with your thumb.

Step 1: Listen to the recorded performance.

Step 2: Play Exercise 18. Start slowly, count aloud and sound the strings where indicated. Increase the tempo only after you've mastered the necessary moves. You should begin to feel the "groove" produced by this approach as you reach a moderate tempo.

Exercise 18

Another syncopation using an A pedal tone in the bass voice is employed in "It's Only a Paper Moon" at measures 44–47. A count is included below the notation in these measures. As an additional preparatory exercise, try following the same counting procedures as suggested for Exercise 18.

About the key changes: At measure 34, "It's Only a Paper Moon" modulates from C major to D major for a second chorus "improve," returning to C major at measure 60 for the final 13 measures. The modulation to D major is accomplished by chromatically ascending octaves: G–G♯–A and is reinforced, starting at measure 34, with the repetition of an A pedal tone in the bass voice.

Approach to self-accompaniment: The melody is supported throughout the arrangement with walking bass lines that outline and imply the chord progression as well as syncopated one-note pedal tones in the bass voice that supply an added kick and groove to the accompaniment.

# IT'S ONLY A PAPER MOON
## (Version 2)

Words by
BILLY ROSE and E.Y. HARBURG
Music by
HAROLD ARLEN
*Arranged by*
*HOWARD MORGEN*

**Freely**
*Intro:*

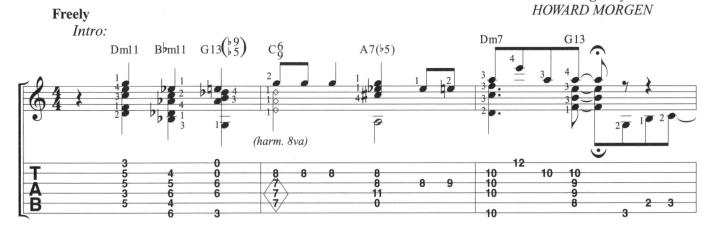

**Moderately, with a beat**
*Chorus:*

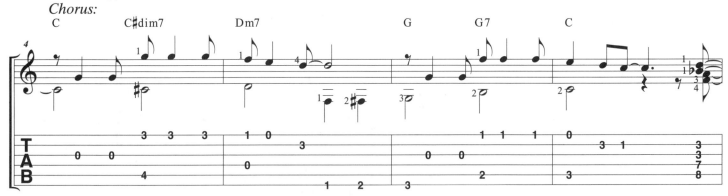

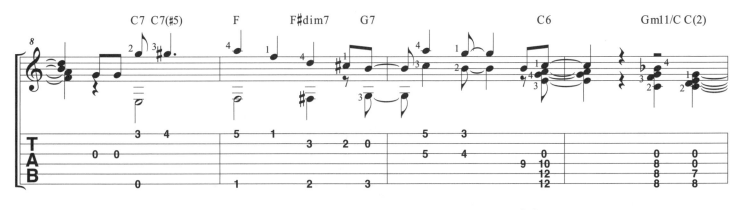

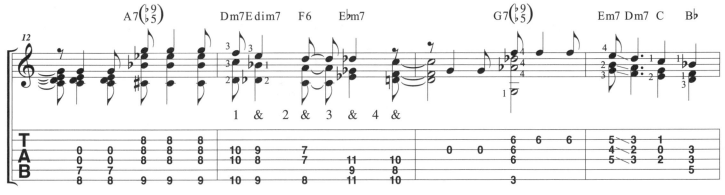

# Guide List for Chapter 14

See the Master Guide List at the end of the book for publisher and item number information for each book.

The following highly recommended folios of contemporary, popular, and jazz standards demonstrate all the harmonic applications, thought processes, and techniques described in Part 2 (Chapters 6 through 11) as well as alternate tunings, choosing original and alternative keys, and modulation (Chapters 12– 14). All the arrangements are written in standard notation and TAB and come with companion CD's.

*Acoustic Masterclass Series: Henry Mancini—Pink Guitar*

*The Wizard of Oz for Solo Guitar,* **Arranged by Mark Hanson**

*Joe Pass Virtuoso Standards: Songbook Collection*

*The Bill Evans Collection for Solo Guitar,* **Arranged by Greg Stone**

*The Gershwin Collection for Solo Guitar,* **Arranged by Howard Morgen**

*The Ellington Collection for Solo Guitar,* **Arranged by Howard Morgen**

*Great Jazz Standards of Duke Ellington,* **Arranged by Fred Sokolow**

# Appendix 1
# Master Guide List

Plan your own course of study from this master guide list of supplementary reading.

*Acoustic Masterclass Series: Henry Mancini—Pink Guitar,* Alfred SAIR009, Book & CD

*All Blues for Jazz Guitar,* Guitar Master Class Pub. MB96842BCD, Jim Ferguson

*All Solos and Grooves,* Guitar Master Class MB99654BCD, Jim Ferguson

*Almanac of Guitar Voice Leading Vols. I & II,* Liquid Harmony Pub. Mr. Goodchord. 1-866-869-5323, Mick Goodrick

*The Art of Solo Guitar Book 1,* Alfred 1053, Book & CD, Jody Fisher

*The Art of Solo Guitar Book 2,* Alfred 1056, Book & CD, Jody Fisher

*Beyond Basics: Introducing Alternate Tunings for Fingerstyle Guitar,* Alfred 907759, DVD, Mark Hanson

*The Bill Evans Collection for Solo Guitar,* Alfred 0426B, Book & CD, Arranged by Greg Stone

*Chord Chemistry,* Alfred EL02778, Ted Greene

*Classic Guitar Technique, Volume I,* Alfred FC01937, Aaron Shearer

*Complete Jazz Guitar Method: Mastering Jazz Guitar: Chord/Melody,* Alfred 14126, Book & CD, Jody Fisher

*Concepts: Arranging for Fingerstyle Guitar,* Alfred TPF0088, Howard Morgen

*Concepts for the Classical and Jazz Guitar,* Jimmy Wyble and Ron Berman, Mel Bay MB97208BCD

*Creative Chord Substitution for Jazz Guitar,* Alfred PMP00047A, Eddie Arkin

*Drop-2 Concept for Guitar,* MB98181, Charles Chapman

*The Ellington Collection for Solo Guitar,* Alfred TGF0036CD, Book & CD, Arranged by Howard Morgen

*Fingerboard Breakthrough (Video),* Howard Morgen, Truefire.com

*Fingerstyle Guitar Standards,* Hal Leonard 699612, Bill Piburn

*Fingerstyle Jazz,* Alfred WMB002

*Fingerstyle Love Songs,* Hal Leonard 699912, Bill Piburn

*George Van Eps Guitar Solos (with TAB),* Mel Bay MB94822 George Van Eps

*The Gershwin Collection for Solo Guitar,* Alfred 0272B, Book & CD, Arranged by Howard Morgen

*Great Jazz Standards of Duke Ellington,* Alfred GF9901CD, Book & CD, Arranged by Fred Sokolow

*Howard Morgen's Solo Guitar (Insights, Arranging Techniques & Classic Jazz Standards),* Alfred 0333B

*Intros and Endings,* MB 20406BCD, Ron Eschete

*Jazz Guitar Chord Bible Complete,* Alfred 0343B, Warren Nunes

*Jazz Guitar for Classical Cats: Chord/Melody,* Alfred 19383, Book & CD, Andrew York

*Jazz Guitar Harmony,* Alfred 20440, Book & CD, Jody Fisher

*Jazz Guitar Standards: Chord Melody Solos,* Alfred WMB011BCD, Book & 2 CDs

*Jimmy Wyble's Solo Collection,* Mel Bay MB 99903BCD, Jimmy Wyble

*Joe Pass Virtuoso Standards: Songbook Collection,* Alfred 0208B

*Just Jazz Real Book,* Alfred FBM0003

*Just Standards Real Book,* Alfred FBM0002A

*Lenny Breau Fingerstyle Jazz,* MB93972, Lenny Breau and John Knowles

*Martin Simpson Teaches Alternate Tunings,* Alfred 20415, Book & DVD

*Mel Bay's Complete Book of Harmonic Extensions,* MB96296BCD, Bret Willmott

*Mel Bay's Complete Book of Harmony, Theory and Voicing,* MB95112, Bret Willmott

*Modern Chord Progressions,* Alfred EL02779, Ted Greene

*Modern Chords Advanced Harmony for Guitar,* MB20440BCD, Vic Juris

*Serie Dedactica para la Guitarra, Cuaderno 2, Technics de la Mano Derecha,* Barry, Buenos Aires

*Solo Jazz Guitar Method,* MB 99509BCD, Barry Greene

*Teaching Your Guitar to Walk,* MB05376BCD, Paul Musso

*The Wizard of Oz for Solo Guitar,* Alfred EL96123, Book & CD, Arranged by Mark Hanson

*Virtuoso Standards: Songbook Collection,* Alfred 0208B, Arranged by Joe Pass

# Appendix 2
# Fingerstyle Applications

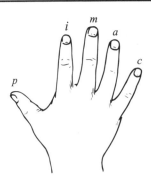

*p* = thumb
*i* = index finger
*m* = middle finger
*a* = anular (ring) finger
*c* = little finger (pinky)

## Basic Strokes and Hand Placement

### Example 1

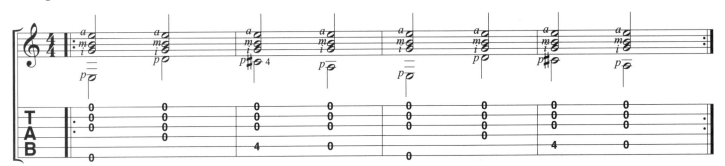

### Example 2

### Example 3

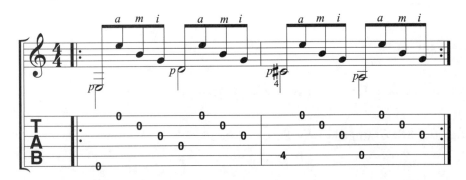

## Exercise 1

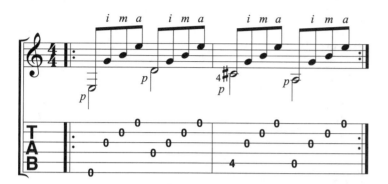

## Exercise 2

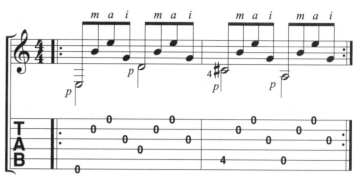

## Exercise 3

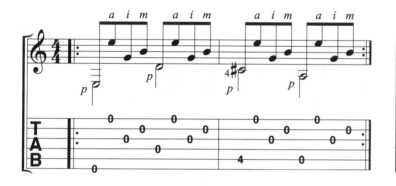

## Exercise 4

## Exercise 5

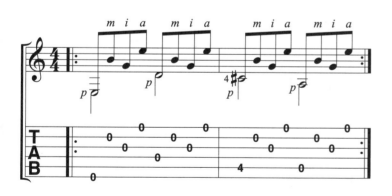

## Exercise 6

# Six Variations

Start with *a*, then *m*, then *i*.

### Variation 1

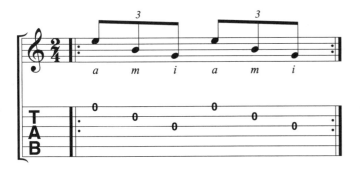

### Variation 2

### Variation 3

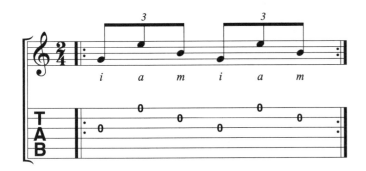

### Variation 4

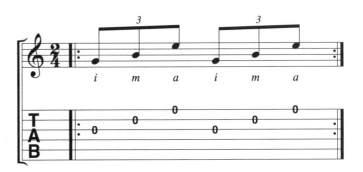

### Variation 5

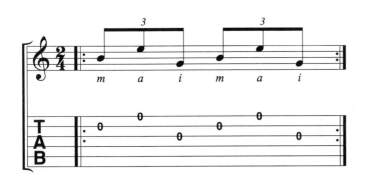

### Variation 6

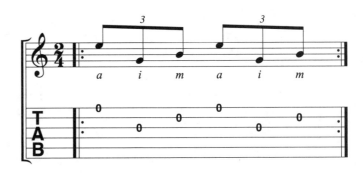

# Six Variations with Added Bass Notes

## Variation 1

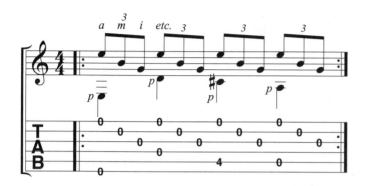

## Variation 2

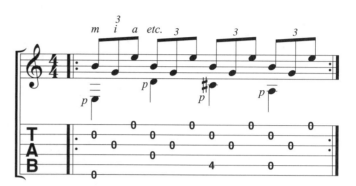

## Variation 3

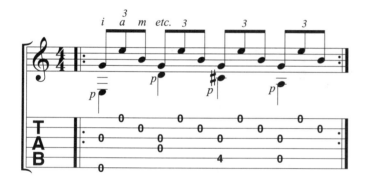

## Variation 4

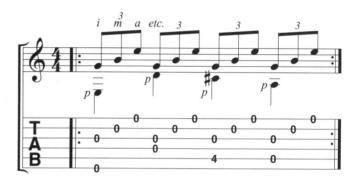

## Variation 5

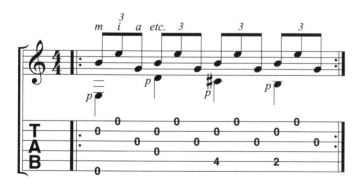

## Variation 6

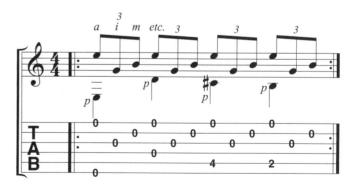

Howard Morgen, guitarist, clinician, and arranger, has written fingerstyle jazz guitar columns and arrangements for *Guitar Player, Guitar World, Acoustic Guitar,* and *Fingerstyle Guitar.* His spectacular solo guitar CD, *Howard Morgen Plays Gershwin,* has won wide critical acclaim, and Howard is currently a columnist for *Just Jazz Guitar* magazine. In addition, Howard is the author of *The Gershwin Collection for Solo Guitar, The Ellington Collection for Solo Guitar, Ten from Guitar Player, Solo Guitar Insights, Fingerstyle Favorites, Concepts,* and *Preparations* (all available from Alfred Publishing); *Paul Simon for Fingerstyle Jazz Guitar* (Amsco Pub.); and *Fingerstyle Jazz Images for Christmas* (Mel Bay). Howard has been a guest artist and instructor at the National Guitar Summer Workshop in Connecticut and has been a faculty member at the Manhattan School of Music, the Guitar Study Center of the New School in Manhattan, and the Jazz Studies Program at the C.W. Post Campus of Long Island University.

Among Howard's students over recent years are singer-songwriter Paul Simon, Edie Brickell, Carly Simon, and Christine Lavin. His bio is included in Maurice Summerfield's *The Jazz Guitar, Its Players and Personalities Since 1900.*

His latest projects include this book, *Through Chord-Melody and Beyond,* and *Fingerboard Breakthrough,* an instructional video from TrueFire.com, also coming out in 2008. For more about Howard, and links to his great publications and videos, go to www.howardmorgen.com.